FROM HERE TO MATERNITY

FROM HERE
TO
MATERNITY

KATHLEEN "CASEY" NULL
CAROLYN SESSIONS ALLEN

Bookcraft
Salt Lake City, Utah

The photographs in this book were taken
by the authors

Library of Congress Catalog Card Number: 86-73043
ISBN 0-88494-619-3

First Printing, 1987

Printed in the United States of America

To mothers everywhere . . .
in every season of maternity

Preface

"It's about time someone told it like it is!" "When I read that story, I cried. Thank you!" "You made me laugh. I'm so glad to know I'm not in this alone!"

These are the kinds of comments we've been getting from people who've read our columns and stories. Before we started writing, we had thought that we were in it alone, too. We had thought that every sister in the ward was "Super Sister," except us. Did we need to pray harder? try harder? give up sleeping altogether?

But as we wrote about our experiences of trying again and again to do our best as resident mothers, wives, and homemakers, and as we spoke to other sisters, we realized that we're all in this together.

And what "this" is, is an incredibly challenging, growing, learning experience.

Certainly the Lord doesn't expect us to be perfect, or perhaps even nearly perfect, parents. If he did, we wouldn't be able to conceive children until we were nearly one hundred years old!

Having children in our twenties to forties means we must work out parenthood while we simultaneously struggle with our own seasons of growth, mistakes, repentance, schooling, careers, and financial stresses.

Surely a wise and superior Being planned a tremendously challenging workshop for us here on earth.

Once we've established a faithful, trusting, and prayerful relationship with our Heavenly Father (who knows our needs and knows our children, even when we can't understand them at all), all we need is the support of our husbands and sisterhood.

Sisterhood is essential because our sisters know what we are experiencing. They have experienced it themselves. Their support fills in when our husbands can't understand or when there is no husband.

As sisters we need to offer each other sincere support. We already bake and cook for each other, and watch each other's children. But also just sharing our real life experiences can be a tremendous support.

Real life is tears of frustration and overwhelming joy. Real life is muddy sneakers and the places they turn up. Real life is love so deep it hurts and hurt so deep that only love can heal. A constant cycle of getting up again to strive for improvement is what real life is all about.

We need each other.

Because all mothers are in this together, we'd like to share a collection of our experiences and feelings as we pass through our maternal seasons.

We hope and pray that as you read this book, you will laugh, cry, recognize yourself, and feel good about the important challenge of motherhood.

Acknowledgments

Thank you:

Kip Emerson Null for saying "How's the book coming?" nearly every day, rather than, "I think this room could stand some dusting."

William R. and Dorothy Hardy for raising me to believe that if I wanted to do something badly enough, I certainly could.

Crismon Lewis and *The Latter-day Sentinel* for being the first to publish me.

Patricia Duenas for being an enthusiastic manuscript reader and critic.

Wayne Ingram and your Way-Lin Graphics for opening your facilities to our photocopying and graphic work.

Jason, Michael, Christopher, and Kiera Null for all the material you provide me in plentiful daily supply.

KATHLEEN "CASEY" NULL

Thank you:

Family, extended and otherwise, for accepting, supporting, and sacrificing in behalf of your wife, mother, daughter, grandmother, aunt, niece, mother-in-law, sister-in-law, and friend. Your names are too numerous to list.

You who have crossed "The Bridge Through the Mist" whose influences have made significant contributions to my maternal season.

CAROLYN SESSIONS ALLEN

Many of the pieces in this book were previously published in *The Latter-day Sentinel*.

Contents

Introduction

To every thing there is a season, and a time to every purpose under the heaven (Ecclesiastes 3:1).

My children were talking about the seasons not long ago. They spoke excitedly about how they would jump in the autumn leaves and build snowmen when winter arrived. They have lived in Huntington Beach for a decade now and have yet to see any fresh fallen snow—on the sand. But I couldn't talk them out of their concept of seasons to be. It seems we need that kind of order to our years. Mothers are no exception.

Being a native Californian, I never really knew what seasons were until my freshman year at BYU.

Oh, we had some snow on the mountains, plenty of rain and fog, and hot smoggy summers, but that's about it. And they tended to get all mixed up anyway.

There'd be a hot, smoggy day on January 1 more often than not, and a foggy, wet day on the last day of school in June.

But usually it was the same old sunshine year round.

Then I traveled across the desert to BYU, not knowing what to expect.

What I discovered were seasons, complete with mountains covered in puffs of color that reminded me of a bowl of Trix. Underfoot were leaves of incredible colors, and the air had an unfamiliar bite to it.

I learned about seasons my freshman year, along with geology, physics, and psychology. Learning to walk on ice, arms laden with books, without slipping took most of the winter semester.

Those days are far behind me now. I often miss the seasons, but while meditating over the vacuum cleaner the other day, I discovered a new way to detect them.

In the realm of homemaking there are but two seasons: Easter basket grass and tinsel. Just about the time you finally rid yourself of the last tenacious strand of tinsel, in march the Easter baskets. And for months the clinging green strands are underfoot, amazingly adept at avoiding the suction of a vacuum cleaner yet mysteriously attracted to any passing toes, to which they adhere themselves like carnivorous green parasites.

When they've finally been conquered, you know that Christmas is just around the corner. And the cycle begins anew with the silver strands.

Ah . . . seasons. The ebb and flow of life.

It's a simplified view, of course, of the seasons as witnessed by a busy mother.

In more serious moments, she realizes that she no longer views the seasons as simply spring with its green Easter basket grass; summer with a houseful of dirty, bare-footed kids and the frogs they caught; autumn with its crisp air and mercifully shorter hours; and winter with unmercifully lengthy Christmas gift lists.

She realizes that she too has her seasons—seasons of mothering. When she nurses her firstborn, when he takes his first steps, and when she daydreams about his future, she is in the spring of her mothering. Her children are fresh buds, she is young—a "green" mother—and everything is new and fresh.

She knows when her summer season arrives. That is when she has a houseful of children, or seemingly so. They may be as young as infants, but they may range in years up to adolescence. This is when the mother is a bit more seasoned, and definitely more fragmented. She will have more commitments outside the home with children involved in more activities such as dances, scouting, athletics, and learning to drive. Yet she may also have a nursing baby and may feel torn between staying home a little longer and keeping up with her older children.

In the autumn of motherhood, her children become independent. They've all entered the educational system, have begun to serve missions, and are beginning, two-by-two, to start their own families. The seasons are not abrupt changes. Her eldest may have a child, and her youngest may still be in grade school. The air becomes more clear, and mothers begin to see their children as independent individuals. This is the season of the harvest when mothers begin to reap joy and sorrow.

Winter is a family time and a tying-up time. In a mother's winter season she is blessed with the enjoyment of posterity to give her warmth. Winter is the time to contemplate and to give to her loved ones. And winter is the time to prepare for renewal.

Motherhood doesn't end here. It goes on forever.

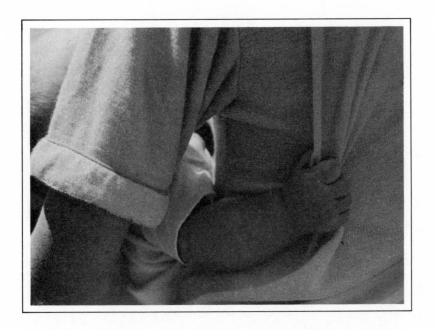

Spring . . .

The beginning of mothering with new "sprouts," new dreams, and new experiences.

On Beginning

That's enough now,
I want to rest.

But you protest
And insist.

You are eager
to go on.

I am tired but
I have no choice.

I am afraid.

I open my eyes in fear.
There are faces hovering by.

I hear soft voices and
feel the overwhelming insistence.

It's time for me to decide—
Shall I let it slide or . . .

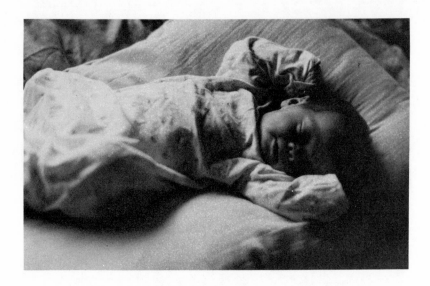

There is much to be done;
I rise up with new strength
and impatient power.

We become a team,
You and I.

Tearing through the veil,
we face death, searing hot.

With all my might
I bring you through
gasping.

"It's a girl!"
The faces cry with joy.

And so do we.

Like life and death, birth experiences are quite different—as different as the individuals we are. Some mothers labor hard with their about-to-be-born. And some mothers make a leisurely appointment . . .

Is This What's Meant by Planned Parenthood?

There are some advantages to a cesarean birth, really. It may eliminate a certain spontaneity associated with child bearing, but it can simplify things.

It is nice to choose, within a week's range, the day of your baby's arrival. For one of mine, I remember trying to decide between "Monday's child who is fair of face," and "Tuesday's child who is full of grace." (I didn't have the luxury of knowing if it was a boy or a girl, so I could have ended up with a graceful football player!)

For another child, I was choosing between Zodiac signs, which I don't really believe in, but it was fun to determine that he would be a Taurus instead of a Gemini. (Now I'm wondering, as I deal with his "bull-headed" personality, if I made the wrong choice!)

Once the date is set, it is nice to pack leisurely and arrive at the hospital organized. There is time to check in, just as if you were checking into a plush hotel. At the prices of hospital rooms, an expensive hotel would be cheaper!

There is time to put things away in your room, just where you want them, and time to get acquainted with your roommate—unless she is heavily sedated or talking on the phone.

Then there's time to relax, sort of, between interns taking medical histories, technicians taking blood and urine samples, and anesthesiologists telling you there's nothing to worry about.

Another advantage is that you can get a jump on writing in the baby book. (And believe me, that's a great advantage, because you're going to be incapacitated after tomorrow.) You can fill out all sorts of information—family tree, doctor's name, fads and customs of the times. Just leave the baby's vital statistics till later. (If you're lucky, you might get them filled in before your child starts school.)

During one of my "vacations," I struck up an acquaintance with a woman in the room next to me. She also was waiting to have a c-section, her first child, and was scheduled for the operation two hours before me.

After visiting hours were over and our husbands had left, I spent a few minutes talking with her. Since I was giving birth to my fourth child, I authoritatively filled her in on all kinds of useful information about child rearing.

The next morning as she was being wheeled out of her room, I wished her good luck. When I asked if she wanted a boy or girl, she answered nervously, "Neither." (I had the distinct feeling that my informative tidbits on the joys of parenthood had caused her to change her mind!)

Perhaps the nicest advantage of a planned cesarean is that it affords time for reflection on the event that is about to take place. I found the following gem in one of my pre-birth mini-journals:

Thoughts on the Eve of the Birth of Our Fourth Child

As we have bustled around trying to finish projects and ready things for the coming of our new baby, we have been caught up in the hurry and scurry of preparing our physical surroundings.

Unfortunately, we haven't taken the time to think about our spiritual readiness.

Tonight I'm alone in my hospital room. The hospital noises have quieted down, and I've had time to reflect on the loftier aspects of tomorrow's events.

The thought came to me that this special spirit that is about to leave our Heavenly Father's presence is also involved in last-minute preparations.

What must it be like to be anticipating the beginning of mortality?

Is he or she hurrying around to say good-bye? Are friends gathering to extend best wishes? Is there a reluctance to leave the security of "over there," and yet an anxiety to pass through the veil?

The baby stirs within my womb as if in answer to my thoughts. I feel an all-consuming oneness with this spirit I'm about to meet.

"Who are you?" I want to ask.

But I already know the answer.

"Help me, Lord," I pray, "to always remember my child's royal lineage."

Not only does our newly born have a royal lineage, he or she comes to us with a distinctive personality very much intact. And very much evident.

It's a Girl!

"It's a girl!" I heard my surprised husband say.

It didn't sink into my postpartum fog for several days. I had heard, "It's a boy!" three times and had expected to hear it once more.

For weeks I caught myself referring to our only daughter, dressed in hand-me-down blue sleepers that were embroidered with "Lil' Slugger," as "he":

"He's awake again already?"

"Look, he's got a double cowlick!"

And then, as I adjusted, as "he—she":

"He—she smiled at Christopher today."

My sister came to the rescue with a box of hand-me-downs from her four daughters.

I put a tiny pink dress on my tiny pink daughter and was awed with the transformation.

"It *is* a girl!" I declared and was promptly swept up in fantasy.

"Let's see, she'll be dainty and cautious and sweet and . . ." Wait a minute.

How could I be so sure?

After three boys, each in their turn, have clung tearfully to my legs, while their Sunbeam teachers pried little fingers loose? After boys with security blankets and various degrees of panic upon sighting a house spider, how can I expect a sugar n' spice girl?

She's a year old now.

When she's had enough to eat, she dumps her plate on the floor with a bone-jarring crash. She climbs slides to the top in the moment it takes to wonder where she went. She examines the teeth and eyes of dogs, waddles after spiders, shoves her brothers out of the way, and goes to bed promptly, wanting nothing to do with rocking, special blankets, thumbs, or any manifestations of security whatsoever.

She's kept us surprised since her arrival, and something tells me there are surprises yet to come.

At least I can count on *that*.

For most of us, it's a real surprise when our children join our family. Just as we thought we might get it all together, they come along. And we discover that as much as we love our little ones, we simply cannot keep up with our former agendas . . . or can we?

Perfecting Motherhood

Well, mothers, are you weary of the well-doing mother you hear lauded from the pulpit every Mother's Day? Have you had it with the guilts?

Not to worry. You need not squirm through another Mother's Day program, or smile sheepishly when you are handed your annual carnation.

Those days are behind you. Yes, you too can be a perfect mother. And you can be perfect, beginning today. Or tomorrow. First of all you must get up three hours before your family does. On Sundays make it five hours. Use those hours to:

— Read your scriptures.
— Pray.
— Exercise.
— Shower or bathe and groom yourself (include full manicure, pedicure, make-up, and hair styling).
— Dress (delete sweat pants, t-shirts, jogging shoes—unless they are new and made of leather; include a freshly starched, lace-edged apron).
— Work in garden (bring a basket outside with you to fill with fresh fruit for breakfast and fresh flowers for the table).
— Prepare hot breakfast.
— Set table with china, crystal, and linen.
— Put home in order.
— Practice musical instrument.
— Wake up family.
— Make beds (check to be certain bed is unoccupied before making; sometimes it is difficult for little ones to get out of a freshly made bed, especially if you use hospital corners).

It is now six o'clock A.M. Time for the family devotional. You will have taught your family to sing various choral arrangements by Handel. There will be at least two family members for each of six parts. Have your five-year-old read a chapter from the Book of

Mormon. This will give you an opportunity to teach patience to your family, by example.

At eight A.M. you will leave the home in an immaculate condition (and that is an important point) with three preschoolers, and the baby in tow to:

— Buy groceries for three weeks.
— Go visiting teaching.
— Purchase fabric to make new covers for living room couch and love seat.
— Take your children to the pediatrician for their weekly checkup.
— Attend a community development meeting, at which you volunteer to chair the "Let's Clean Up Our City" committee.

You'll be home by nine-thirty and will have time to put away the groceries, make the couch and love seat covers, and play chess with your children before you eat a hot lunch together (you are teaching them table etiquette), and put them into their beds for a nap.

While they nap, you can wash eight loads of laundry, iron it, put it away, put up wallpaper in the dining room, harvest some vegetables from the garden for dinner, make a quilt, and wash the lunch dishes.

While dinner is cooking, you really must prepare a family home evening lesson with visual aids, a Mother Education lesson for Relief Society on Sunday, and make the beds again.

After dinner, the family can practice their parts on the Bach piece you are working on, while everyone washes the dishes.

At family home evening you could follow up the lesson with a lesson in oil painting, ballet, or fencing. Then the family can meet in the family room for dessert—crepes suzette or Baked Alaska which you made at one o'clock A.M. that morning.

Once the family is tucked in you'll need to stay up for five or six more hours. This will give you the opportunity to bake a loaf of bread for the sister who just had a baby, hem your daughter's skirt, crochet a cap and mittens for your son who is on a mission in Norway, mop the floor, color code the family's socks, weed the strawberries, bake cookies for your son's first grade field trip, write in your journal, make granola for breakfast in the morning, and iron tomorrow's apron.

Try to get to bed before two o'clock A.M. After all, it will be a quarter of three before you know it, and time to begin another day.

On the other hand, maybe you'd rather settle for just being a *good* mother and get a little shut-eye.

Let It Flow

My daughter is only two years old and already she has a tremendously impressive collection of baby dolls.

With no role model of a mother and baby, and no big sister to emulate, she is nevertheless a busy little mother. She rocks her babies; she tucks them into bed. She scolds them and soothes them. She bathes them, and she tells them to lie down. When one of them lost an eye, the loving concern flowed freely to envelop the afflicted baby. She didn't love her any less for being one-eyed.

I am amazed watching her. How did she learn so much nurturing behavior? She's the youngest and only daughter. I learn from her that mothering can be natural, if you just let it flow.

Birth is but a beginning, not a conclusion. Baptism, or rebirth, is like that too. It's a beginning. After that fresh start, it's up to us.

We give birth to our children, and then, we lead them to the water.

On Baptism and Birth

My husband can only observe as I
birth our son . . .

As he emerges from the water,
fresh and pure

My power is ages old, passed on through
generations of mothers.

> And I can only observe as my husband
> baptizes him . . .
>
> > As he emerges from the water,
> > fresh and pure
>
> My husband's power is ages old, passed on through
> generations of righteous men.

One of the most important maternal roles is that of teacher. It is our gentle teaching that leads our children to the waters of baptism, and to an understanding of its significance. But from the moment of birth our children also teach us.

Human Contact

I have tipped over Christopher's toy basket and kneel beside him while he mouths and chews and fingers and shakes the various toys. Seeing him occupied, I move to the other side of the room to work. Immediately Christopher crawls across the room to play with my feet, grab my legs, and try to climb into my lap.

Christopher teaches me that things are okay but human contact is better.

In the spring of motherhood we give just about all we've got to the care of our newborn, and then neglect to give credit where credit is due.

Service

My friend's testimony inspired the "guilts" in me. She was thanking half the ward for the kindness they had shown her family during their period of crisis. She thanked some for meals, some for child care, and some for hauling out and returning mountains of laundry. The members of the ward beamed back at her. I squirmed.

What crisis? I wondered. I was sadly, guiltily uninformed. Why hadn't she told me she needed help?

I berated myself. It was up to me to find out, wasn't it? Did I forget to say, "How are you?" Then she could reply, "Oh, our family is in the midst of a horrendous crisis, but other than that, we're fine."

Admittedly, I had been out of touch because I'd just been through a recent crisis of my own—a new baby. But that didn't soothe my feelings of guilt. I went home feeling that I wasn't doing my share of service, and I needed to do something about it.

But I had three boys to feed, bathe, dress, clean up after, read a story to, and get to bed, along with caring for the newborn baby. She was hungry every time she was conscious, wet every time she wasn't, and crying most of the time in between. I didn't have time to think of how I could serve others.

Yet the thought that I must serve persisted.

At last, with the boys in bed, I nursed, rocked, changed, nursed, and soothed the baby, finally putting her to bed.

It was about eleven o'clock when I finally had them all tucked in—or so I thought—and I eased my weary body into bed with a sigh of relief.

The baby began to cry. I waited. *Does she mean it?* She meant it. I sighed another kind of sigh and pulled myself back up to rock and soothe and nurse some more.

Contented at last, she curled up with her knees tucked under. I paused to watch her for a quiet moment. My legs ached, and I realized that I'd been on my feet all day—even throughout the testimony meeting.

Just as I was about to renew my lament about not having the time to serve others, I was interrupted by a powerful feeling that seemed to fill the room. I felt as if there were angelic beings watching over my daughter, and that they were aware of my thoughts. They seemed to let me know, without words, that I was performing a valuable service. They were aware of my round-the-clock service to my family. I felt that they were encouraging and reminding me, "When ye are in the service of your fellow beings [even your own family] ye are only in the service of your God." (From the June 1986 *Ensign*. Used by permission.)

Perhaps we occasionally feel guilty about our involvement in serving within our families because it can be so nourishing to our souls. There is peace to be found in turning off all external stimuli and observing our own newborn who is just discovering the world.

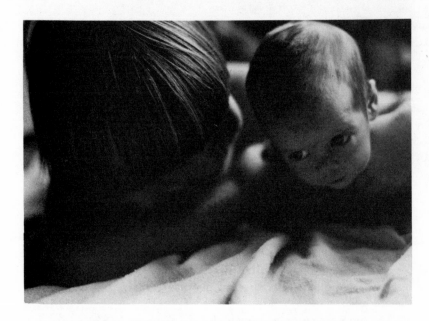

Brand New

Three-month-old Christopher looks out of the window at the sky and makes high squeaky sounds. After a puzzled moment I realize that he's imitating the sounds of the birds he hears!

Oh, Christopher, teach me to hear the birds again. You are hearing, seeing, and touching with the intensity of a brand new human being. I have forgotten, and don't perceive as sensitively as you. Let me watch how you do it, and maybe I'll remember as I share your experiences with you.

We want our children to grow and increase their capabilities, but we must be ever one step ahead of their abilities.

Lament

Alas, alack,
and woe is me;

There goes my
precious privacy.

Go get my things
and store them high;

Hurry, now,
the time is nigh.

Move those shelves,
Guard those drawers—

My daughter's learned
to open doors.

As teaching parents we are ever mindful of the capabilities and foibles of our individual children. But as they reach the age where others begin to share that role with us, we must keep in mind that unrelated teachers have no such advantage. For example:

Dear Primary Teacher

Dear Primary Teacher,

My very young son is in your class. Let me tell you about him.

He likes to say his prayers, but if he is asked to pray in front of others he will efficiently bless the food. So if you call on him to pray in class and hear him express gratitude for the food, thank him anyway. One day someone besides me will hear one of his eloquent and charming prayers; hopefully it will be you.

He is also very affectionate. Although he is a bit young to have such a preference for girls, and not old enough to have an aversion to them, I'd suggest that you seat him by other boys. He likes to kiss girls and wrestle with boys. I think you might be better prepared for wrestling boys than a lot of kissing.

Please keep in mind that three-year-olds have incredible imaginations. Don't believe a word he says about our personal family life.

Although we will frisk him before he enters your classroom, the inevitable Lego or ball bearing will get through anyway. Simply

reassure him that his treasures will be returned to him soon as you slip them into your pocket.

You may need to remind him that he is to remain fully clothed until he gets home.

He will raise his hand and volunteer for anything. Please help him see that anyone can raise their hand, the important part is carrying it out.

Sometimes he will miss class because he is hovering between babyhood and childhood. Please don't be offended. It takes time to let go of Mom and take the hand of a teacher.

He will cry in class from time to time. Don't be alarmed. He needs to find out if you can comfort him.

Although at home he has moments when he is careful and contemplative, in your classroom he is likely to be silly and scribble all over your handouts. Even three-year-olds are self-conscious and hide their true selves in a group situation.

A gentle touch from you and an encouraging word will assure him that he belongs. You will be rewarded by his devotion.

You may think he isn't learning a thing in your class with all the wrestling, kissing, scribbling, silliness, and undressing. But he is, I assure you. He remembers every word you say, every facial expression you make, every attitude you imply.

He is so young. He doesn't yet know what classrooms are all about. He is a tender stranger to adults who are not family members. Please keep in mind when he tips his chair over or has a tantrum because another boy got the brown crayon first, that he has only been on earth for three years. And he has so much to learn. And that parents who love him beyond his comprehension have entrusted him to your influence.

Lucky is the mother who, upon moving from early motherhood to a more "seasoned" state, learns what it takes to be the right kind of mother—and realizes she has what it takes, and always did.

Mother's Day Shouldn't Be Guilt Day

For many of us, Mother's Day could just as easily be called National Guilt Day.

We sit in pews, hankies in hand. Our tears are for those wonderful mothers we hear about that we still emulate.

We look around us, for we are certain those other mothers in attendance are the ones who are the appropriate recipients of all that praise and adoration.

For me it began even before the birth of my first child. Only a few months along, I attended the traditional Sunday Mother's Day meetings, my dress straining under the pressure of expansion.

When the young men in the ward began to pass out the pink carnations, I began to be nudged.

"Stand up! Stand up!"

I didn't.

I couldn't.

I knew those tributes and flowers were not intended for me. And somehow I knew that next year I would, of course, be that mother they described and I would proudly stand and accept a carnation.

I continued to attend on succeeding Mother's Days, but I never could figure out who that mother was that was honored from the pulpit each year. I dutifully accepted my flower or booklet, my consolation prize.

After all, these tributes were presented on Sunday, and if my family and I were in attendance at all, even with mismatched socks and unruly cowlicks, I didn't get them there on time by singing lullabies and gently sponging apple cheeks.

Then I began to think of this wonderful mother as a symbol, not unlike the familiar, ageless, motherly baker whose face appears on all those boxes of cake mix. She's a masthead of maternity. A goal.

I would leave my meetings on those Sundays full of resolve. I must bake, sing, and speak softly much more . . .

But I never did.

And now Mother's Day is here again.

My son just handed me a card he made in school. It was flowery and sticky (literally). On the outside it says,

"I Love You, Mommy, because . . ."

Here it comes. The moment of truth. I opened the card.

". . . you like to ride on roller coasters."

You mean after all these years of thinking I must bake more cakes and trying to be a perfect mother, I never realized I could be a perfectly acceptable mother just by doing what I like to do anyway?

To perfectly acceptable mothers everywhere: Happy Mother's Day!

Not only are imperfect mothers perfectly acceptable, they are people, too—imperfect people who are striving and doing.

Mothers Are People

Mothers are people who get so used to taking care of a batch of children that they forget that it takes about fourteen hours a day to do it. And that's why the great new recipes go untried, the needlework pillow remains unfinished, and the visual aids for homemaking meeting are finished at two o'clock A.M.

Mothers are people who are deeply grateful for whatever sleep they get.

Mothers are people whose dressy shoes and earrings get dusty and whose red nail polish is used to mark toxic substances, but who can still remember the importance of dressy shoes, earrings, and red nail polish.

Mothers are people who get called back to school, called back to the crib, called from work to pick up a suit at the cleaners, and called just about everything but their first name.

Mothers are people who depend on telephones, baby-sitters, microwaves, and velcro.

Mothers are Primary presidents, Relief Society presidents, room mothers, and den mothers because someone once said, "If you want it done right, ask a busy person."

Mothers are people who feel responsible for the atmosphere in the home, the condition of the carpets, the nutrition of their family, the spiritual upbringing of their children, their family's hygiene, their children's grades, their husband's happiness, and their dog's rabies shots. And when mothers collapse with the flu, they drag themselves out of bed to take care of the atmosphere, the carpets, the nutrition, the spiritual upbringing, the hygiene, the grades, the husband, and the dog anyway.

Mothers are former litte girls who loved flowers, ribbons, sweet smells, and delicate things, and ended up with snakes and hamsters, dirty sweat socks, and green ooze coming out from under the refrigerator.

Mothers are people who are honored once a year with platitudes and orations and flowers. And the following day they get back to real life again.

Mothers are poets, painters, bookkeepers, beekeepers, musicians, and magicians who share a silken thread of wondrous biology.

Mothers are people with peaceful havens for laps, healing kisses, and the incredible ability to cook from a recipe while listening to one child's tale of woe and another's spelling practice.

Mothers are coronated at the birth of their first child. And they continue to wear the crown, dim or bright, heavy or light, forever after.

Mothers are people who like to garden. Well, many of them do anyway. And anyone who gardens knows just how much work it is to raise a crop from those little sprouts.

How Does My Garden Grow?

There was a time when I was known far and wide for my way with houseplants. They were lush and green, and I misted them and checked them for mealybugs daily.

Those days are but a mist of a memory now.

My green thumb has browned as surely as those plants. My brown thumb jinxes anything that grows in the ground.

With my first unborn child growing at record speed, I contorted in the garden plot my husband cleared for me. He even brought me those little plants that are already thriving. I planted them in a neat row, then straightened my aching back to view my work. The next

morning when I looked out of the window I saw a neat row of green stems instead of the bright pansies I had put there. Somewhere in the yard there were some bloated snails sleeping off a binge.

With my first child outgrowing his clothes and the second kicking at me with a fury to be born, I misted a Boston fern in our rain forest bathroom. It started to turn brown. It shriveled and died.

With my first child marching off to school with his rock collection, my second wearing hand-me-downs from the first, and the third playing basketball—in utero—while awaiting his turn to join his brothers, I planted tomatoes. The tomatoes actually ripened. When they were finally ready I found that every insect inhabiting the neighborhood had beat me to them.

With my first child marching off to school with his "ghetto blaster," my second marching off to school with his stamp collection, and my third watching Sesame Street in hand-me-downs from who knows, and the fourth kicking me in the diaphragm while waiting to blossom forth, I planted tulip bulbs. I carefully followed the directions and even measured the holes with a ruler to be sure they were planted correctly. They never showed. That was two years ago and we haven't seen so much as a sprout. My husband says he'll make tombstones for all the bulbs I've buried in the yard.

But my daughter *did* burst forth in a great flurry.

Come to think of it, the more children I've sprouted, the more brown my thumb has become.

So I've given up the practice of growing things in dirt. That was just a stepping stone, you might say, on my way to growing human beings.

I practiced nurturing and repotting. Now I'm nurturing and re-bedding. I'm pinching back to avoid wild little sprouts. I'm misting with tears and laughter. I'm feeding, turning, polishing. Instead of mealybugs I'm looking for flaws in self-esteem. Instead of root rot I'm searching for inadequate ways of relating. I'm supplying water, sunshine, love, kisses, and peanut butter and honey.

And maybe, someday, I'll be known again for my garden—my garden of generations.

Summer . . .

Hazy, crazy days; young, active, curious children—beginning to test their wings . . . and their mothers.

The summer season of mothering is like the summer season of the year. It's almost more than a mother can endure and it's exactly where she wants to be.

You Get It from Your Kids

Watch out parents! You may be more neurotic than you think! As the popular saying states, "Insanity is hereditary—you get it from your kids."

My father is a retired psychologist, and I grew up being familiar with the plethora of tests utilized by professionals in the field. Recently I had the opportunity to look over a popular personality assessment that requires the client to answer with either a "true" or "false." No explanations, just "true" or "false."

I began to wonder if I would be promptly taken away if I were to answer those questions literally . . . as a parent.

For instance, the test states:

"I often see strange animals that others can't see."

I'd have to answer "true." The other day I was on the phone trying to arrange some visiting teaching when three boys walked huddle-fashion across the kitchen floor to get a jar from the cup-board. I continued my conversation, "I could go next Wednesday after two o'clock P.M. if you're free then."

It was then that I realized they were huddled around some kind of ambiguous amphibious creature and whatever it was, it was dripping muddy water on the floor. I said into the telephone, "You wouldn't believe the strange creature I see dripping on the floor . . . but . . . well, three o'clock would be just fine."

And what about this one? "I am often disturbed in my sleep."

Of course I am.

And there's, "Are you afraid of germs on doorknobs?"

True. Well, maybe not germs but certainly peanut butter.

"Do you feel a need to wash your hands frequently?"

Absolutely. I've got two in diapers!

"Do you sometimes feel helpless?"

True. Summertime, Easter vacation, and Christmas vacation.

Then they have, "I often hear noises in the night."

True. Newborns, nocturnal bathroom visitors, croupy coughers, teeth grinders, sleep talkers, nightmare criers, and bodies that fall out of bunkbeds and go thump in the night.

Here's a good one, "I think someone may be trying to poison me."

Well, maybe not intentionally. But I am a little paranoid. I always check glasses before using them. You just never know. I found one today that had held fresh bait only hours before! I'm talking about worms!

Then there's "I often forget where I put things."

Either that or they sprout legs and take off on their own. What if I put *that* down on a personality test?

I can just see a roomful of bearded psychoanalysts going over my test with a lot of serious *hmmm*'s.

But the test just doesn't ask enough. I'd surely need to add a note: "My sleep is disturbed. I'm fatigued. I check glasses before drinking from them, and I wipe doorknobs before using them. I can't find *anything*. I can't hear myself think. I see strange creatures, hear strange sounds night and day. I'm ready for baskets . . . but don't you dare come to take me away!

"I'm staying right here."

In the summer of our maternity we seem to be at our busiest. That's when we most need to be receptive to the lessons our children can teach us concerning what life is really about.

Michael Sings

Michael sings . . . everyday. Everyday at the top of his lungs!

Here we are in the same environment. We both have our problems. His are just as real and important to him as mine are to me.

I see dirty laundry, a pile of bills, and no relief in sight.

Michael has conflicts with his brothers, a class to attend in which he knows no one, bumps, scrapes, chores to do, and wild hair that embarrasses him.

Yet I grouch, "Hurry up. Stop it. Clean this up!" All day I grouch. And Michael sings.

I need to be more like Michael.

Sleeping children present an opportunity to accomplish everything that can't possibly be done when they are so vibrantly awake. Even that opportunity, however, like all good things, must come to an end.

Mothers, you heard it here first. There is no more time. There will never be enough time. We already have all there is. Is there no hope?

Beating the Clock

Who cares about rubies and diamonds? The most precious commodity I know of is time. Is there ever enough of it?

When I hear someone say, "We all have the same amount, twenty-four hours: it's what we do with it . . ." I want to wrestle them to the ground in midsentence and pin them to the floor until they gasp "Uncle!"

Then I wouldn't let them up until they promised to hear my version of that overrated twenty-four hours.

Sure, we each start out with twenty-four hours, but there are petty thieves in my midst. Days and weeks sometimes go by without an hour to call my own.

The biggest time burglars I know make the telephone, meetings, housework, yard work, and tax forms look like amateurs. These time thieves are juveniles. My own children, juvenile delinquents.

Consider the years of looking after each child's bottom until he or she finally figures out how to do it alone. And that's just the tip of the iceberg.

In order to save time during these child-dominated years, I'd have to inherit a nanny and add on a children's wing (in Wyoming?).

The odds are against that. Besides, I kind of like those cute little bottoms. But twenty-four hours is simply never enough time!

I know all about time management. I am becoming an expert. If I live to tell about it, the world some day will be lined up at my doorstep waiting to glean a tidbit of time management wisdom as I pass.

I can shampoo four heads—two straight, one wavy, and one extra curly—in two minutes.

I jump on the trampoline while I talk on the phone, which makes my callers think I am vibrant and enthusiastic.

I do the breakfast dishes while I am eating. Unfortunately, one morning my toast emerged soggy from a long cycle in the silverware tray.

I clean up the bathroom while I'm showering; doesn't everybody?

I never do one thing at a time, and I'm trying to find a way to sleep faster, hopefully aerobically, so I can get that out of the way, too.

I am my own boss (I think), a free-lancer. I accept assignments from editors, company presidents, schools, bishops, Relief Society boards, Kip, Jason, Michael, Christopher, and Kiera (oh, they're my family—the most demanding deadline I've got).

Why don't I chuck it all and sail to New Zealand? There are days . . . But I love everything I do. I don't want to do less. My problem is that I want to do more.

There are twenty-four hours for each of us. But it's not enough for me. And I know what I need to solve my problem. If only it could be managed.

I need a wife! (Okay, a clone?)

Perhaps we wouldn't feel so rushed if we could learn to feel the joy and love in even the simplest things that we do, the way children often do.

Joy and Love

Whenever I go to change Christopher's diaper, Michael is right there, underfoot, holding Christopher's hand, chattering to him, "helping" me.

It drives me nuts and I want to send him away.

But I say to myself, "Michael, you are teaching me about joy and love. You rejoice in comforting your brother and helping me. You have a sixth sense that sends you running to the changing table from other rooms at changing time."

Now I need to learn patience and not be in such a hurry to step on you, squashing your exuberant expression of joy and love.

Often the standards for judging "mothering performance" are blatantly superficial. If your child is eating watercress sandwiches on homemade sour dough bread with her hair in French braids and her toys alphabetized, you are deemed a good mother. But there is no way to measure how much real mothering is taking place. Real mothering takes time; don't waste another moment.

A "Real" Mother

Well, Mother's Day is here again. No more of this "perfect mom" stuff, it's time we figured out what a real mother is.

So to make it official, here's a list of what a real mother is and does:

A real mother thinks her child is the brightest and most beautiful child in the world.

A real mother irons only the parts of clothing that will be showing—like cuffs, collars, and the one side that will be facing the audience in the Primary program.

A real mother uses garlic powder even though she owns two garlic presses.

A real mother uses Velcro whenever possible.

A real mother closes the door to her children's bedroom and is not even tempted to clean it up just a little before the team gets back from soccer practice.

A real mother cries when her child goes to kindergarten, whether it is her oldest or her seventh baby.

A real mother "lets" her children walk home from school when she could give them a ride.

A real mother doesn't wipe off a peanut butter kiss . . . until the kisser is out of sight.

A real mother wakes up a child who forgot to feed his cat before he went to bed.

A real mother is tolerant of a little mess, a little noise, and a little confusion . . . but just a little.

A real mother insists upon and glories in nap time.

A real mother takes shortcuts wherever possible when it comes to cooking and cleaning. Because then she has time to: teach shoelace tying, praying, and reading; wash faces; read stories; take nature walks; kiss boo-boos; push swingers; hold the hands of roller skaters; provide baking soda for science projects; trim bangs; picnic; hug; sing songs; dream dreams; and provide the raw materials for a life's supply of childhood memories.

A real mother, forsaking much else, does a lot of real mothering.

Polishing Dreams

Let me introduce myself.

I am the keeper of the house and home.

I am the sweeper of sand, after a "childful" day of giggling at the beach,

The washer of strawberry-stained rompers.

For a homeful of future,
I am the duster of dreams,
The polisher of aspirations.
I vacuum disappointments and kiss away failures.

And at night . . .
When they're all tucked in for rest
Upon a cushion of silence,
I take out my dreams.
I examine, sort, and polish them
till they gleam in the night;
And I drift off to sleep in the glow . . .
My night light.

We can't examine the seasons of maternity without a close look at the men in our lives. Where would we be without them?

A New Breed of Dads

There are unsung heroes in our midst. A new breed of father. Without fanfare, they have been volunteering for the frontlines of family life.

Let us recognize them lest they spend their courage in vain.

They are the fathers who are not only marching deliberately into labor and delivery rooms, they are coaching labor and "catching" their offspring.

They have opinions on bottle versus breastfeeding and discuss them with other fathers while bouncing a baby on their knees in priesthood meeting.

They bravely march forward to change any kind of diaper without a single derogatory comment to hinder troop morale.

They are fearless and offer no feeble excuses to avoid battle, such as, "I can't put the dishes away; I don't know where they go."

They are confident in enemy territory—equally at ease in the principal's office, pediatrician's waiting room, and parent-teacher conferences.

They are willing and able to upgrade their training, to go into battle better armed. They read Dobson and Ginott and say to their two-year-olds, "Do you want oatmeal in the blue bowl or oatmeal in

the yellow bowl?" What they feel like saying is, "Look here, buster! You're gonna have oatmeal if I have to serve it to you on your head!"

They never let the unit down. If they are finished with their assignments and see that their first mate is still fighting a mighty battle, they call in reinforcements and help sort those 162 sweat socks with 114 different versions of red and blue stripes.

They are capable of leading the unit when their wives are taken away to other battles, such as roadshow practice, homemaking meetings, and Primary activity days.

If they are the first to arrive on the scene of casualties—whether it be a five-pound jar of peanut butter shot down over linoleum, or a two-year-old who had too many spins in a tree swing—they do not retreat. They squelch squeamishness and march onward.

Let's set aside a day to honor these brave men.

Instead of the traditional loud tie or loud cologne for Father's Day, why not a purple heart?

There's an art to fathering. Fathers have their own style. Often it is to appear stern and firm. And often it works. At least it fools the kids, most of the time.

A Crusty Father's Day

Men. Rough, tough, macho. Or so their children think.

Fathers are men who sternly tell their children that, "It is bedtime now, no ifs, ands, or buts; and I don't want to hear another sound unless it is your head hitting your pillow," because they've been waiting all day for a chance to play with the new race car set that glows in the dark.

Fathers are men who firmly admonish the youngster who decided to paint her face while getting ready for church with red felt-tip pens—calling it "make-up"—to wash her face. Then they dissolve into laughter when she is out of earshot.

Fathers are men who insist that their sons dress properly for the Sabbath, and find their scriptures "or else," and then get something in their eye when a son gives a talk or bears his testimony.

Fathers are men who declare, "You are grounded for the next

twenty-five years, or until you clean up your room, whichever comes first!" Then later they turn to their wives and ask, "Do you think I was too hard on him?"

Fathers are men who inspire in their children a wide spectrum of reactions from, "[tearfully] Daddy says I can't watch TV again for as long as I live, and I don't think that's fair!" to, "Daddy says we're all going to go to the beach today and have hot dogs and I can't wait!" all within the same twenty-four hours.

Fathers are men with a crusty outer shell that envelops a tender heart. Fathers fool very few for very long. To crusty fathers everywhere, a tender Father's Day.

Fathers are usually away from home too much to observe their children's daily activities.

Perhaps it's not necessary; they were, after all, little boys once.

Perhaps it's really we mothers who need to be reminded that the world won't cave in if our carrot cake does and that there is so much amusement to be found anywhere we might look.

Amusement

Jason comes inside and shows me the "dog prints" he has collected (neighborhood dogs, stamp pad, and notebook). He describes the taking of a print: "He didn't mind, he just stood there . . ."

Jason teaches me about curiosity—"I wonder what a dog print would look like?"—and about creative innovation. He doesn't ask me for stamps to use with his new stamp pad; he uses what is available and he's not limited by convention. He teaches me about trying and risk taking: "What if the dog doesn't like it, what if he tries to bite me?"

And he teaches me to find amusement in life.

It seems that if parents want a little amusement, a little R and R, or just a little night off, they must plan a strategy that would outmaneuver Alexander the Great and all his armies.

There's just no getting around it. The kids are nearly always underfoot. Spouses, with so many duties to fulfill, can quickly become just "ships that pass in the night." Usually one is going to bed after finally getting the baby to bed and the other is getting up to go to work. Are we amused yet?

It's not only important to keep on dating, it's imperative. Any kind of date will do.

Ah, Alone!

My husband and I went out on a date the other night.

That's newsworthy.

We don't often have such an opportunity, what with six jobs, four Church callings, and four children between the two of us.

But we went. We actually walked out on all that and went to dinner and a movie.

It's not the same as it was when we were single. There was no time for the car-washing, hair-curling, and fancy-dressing rituals.

There wasn't even time to change. We just slipped out of the door in jeans and running shoes, grateful for the chance.

Our baby-sitter, however, was nicely groomed.

I must admit that we did stop off at a shopping center to pick up some laundry detergent and baby cereal. You might think that's not a very romantic thing to do on a date, but hand holding in the condiments aisle can be wonderful . . . comparatively.

At the restaurant we felt funny. It was almost boring just sitting, talking, and eating. Boring but nice. We sat at the edge of our seats, ready for disaster, out of habit. If anyone had choked on food, we would've been the first to assist.

In the booth next to us there was a kid who reminded us of our three-year-old.

After dinner we browsed around some shops while waiting for our movie to begin. I kept looking behind me as I walked, and my husband looked at me strangely but didn't say anything.

Once I even blurted out, "Hurry up, there's a car coming!" Then he *really* looked at me strangely.

We looked in windows.

"Oh, wouldn't that be perfect for Kiera?"

"Yes, and wouldn't the boys love that?"

At one point I dropped my purse. It was so light without the usual diapers, bottles, burp rags, cars, and trucks that I forgot I had it.

"Oopsie!" I exclaimed, before I could stop myself.

"Oopsie"? I got the strangest look then.

One of the boys in the film reminded us of our eldest. The baby in the film was the same age as our baby.

After the film we tried not to talk about the kids, so we critiqued the film, the actors, and the plot. We discovered symbolism to discuss. We correlated the film's message with contemporary thought. As we approached our street we grew silent.

Inside, all were angelically sleeping except the baby. She leaped up at seeing us walk in the door.

Later we debated over the second best part of the evening.

We were unanimous about the best part—coming home.

Ah, coming home. Such a sweet joy. The kind of joy that lasts— until it is time to do the laundry again, that is.

Washday Joys

I have a friend who has trained her children to do their own laundry. At first I thought it was a great idea, and envied her in-genuity and persistence.

However, I was teaching my twelve-year-old how to do a load that "just had to be done" so she could wear a special outfit to school tomorrow, and began to realize what a complicated process laundry can be.

It has become such a habit over the years that most of us don't give laundry a second thought, and usually plan a Primary or Relief Society lesson while we sort the week's clothes.

"No," I explained to her, "you cannot wash the hot pink blouse with the white undies unless you don't mind turning them pink." She didn't really care about the underwear, but she drew the line at the white sweatshirt and opted for a second load. Luckily, our washing machine has one of those mini-baskets designed especially for families with teenagers.

By the time I had explained the merits of washing in cold water versus warm water, water level, soaps to use for warm and cold loads, which things needed a detergent booster, and a seeming myriad other details, I felt as if I'd done a dozen commercials for various laundry products.

(I've advised my daughters that an advanced chemistry class is a prerequisite for being a mother—and for more reasons than knowing how to handle all the chemicals involved in laundering!)

I decided it really is easier to do it myself—often a mother's excuse for not teaching her children the things they need to know.

Besides, as I did the laundry this morning, I took note of the benefits I could glean from this otherwise mundane activity. I didn't necessarily have sweet nostalgic thoughts pass through my mind about each family member as I sorted his or her dirty socks, but I did notice what a good chronicler of the week's activities the laundry hamper was.

Since I am a Monday laundress, the first layer of clothing reflects our Sunday activities. Shirts, slacks, and dresses only worn for three hours sometimes can be retrieved and hung on hangers without washing. This saves time and expense, not to mention the wear and tear on the clothes.

Saturday's layer is usually the most interesting and would give someone who didn't know us a clue as to what we are like. Grimy gardening clothes indicate a farmer in our household, while an assortment of soccer and baseball uniforms, swimming suits, sweats, and shorts leaves no doubt that we are an athletic family.

Also in the weekend strata are items from Friday and Saturday night diversions befitting the season. Light play clothes during the summer, with even an extra dress shirt for occasional youth dances, might appear. Or sweat shirts and jeans could indicate football season is at hand. A layer of sand is a sure sign that the beach was on the weekend agenda.

Digging deeper down in the hamper, the rest of the week is often jumbled together because invariably someone puts something in at the first of the week and decides near the end of the week that it probably could be worn again. Looking for the desired item mixes the hamper contents considerably. (After all, people are supposed to stir their compost piles!)

Sprinkled throughout the week's wash are various leotard and tights outfits, which could lead an outsider to the conclusion that a dance troupe resides at our address. This clue is a little misleading since there is only one daughter living at home now. However, she takes three types of dance lessons and has to have a different outfit for each. Sometimes I even get into the leotard act with an aerobics class.

Look at all the fun my friend is missing, I thought to myself as I heaped the various piles on the floor of the laundry room. Besides, I get lots of exercise on Mondays running up and down the stairs from my word processor to the washing machine—it's healthy.

Topping it all off are the pocket surprises. Long ago I broke my children of leaving money in their pockets by claiming it as "finders-keepers." Doing the laundry isn't nearly as lucrative anymore, although once in a while they forget. I really hit the jackpot one time with my oldest son's entire wallet!

I still find the things that most moms find: "interesting" notes that probably weren't meant for Mom's eyes; a variety of pencils, crayons, and marking pens (that makes me glad I'm doing the wash, because the kids would probably miss them, and we all know what a red crayon can do to ruin your day, not to mention the dryer and everything in it); candy and gum wrappers (sometimes with the gum and candy still in them—a sweet bonus); small toys, including innumerable Legos; and other treasures stored for safe keeping.

The best pocket surprises usually occur near Mother's Day or Christmas, and although they are crumpled and folded into a jillion folds, their sentiment brings a tear to any mom's eye. "I love you, Mom. Happy Mother's Day." Or "Merry Christmas, Mom and Dad —I love you." Maybe not very original, but priceless all the same. (I wonder if my friend's children are better at delivering important papers?)

Although I still do the washing, I realized years ago that folding the laundry could be a family affair. I even pay if I have to. Several of my offspring have discovered that they can do it while watching afternoon cartoons—a great way to earn a little money.

On days when everyone is bogged down with too much homework or for one reason or another I don't have any takers on folding the laundry, I leave it on the kitchen table. The rule is that we can't eat dinner until all the clothes are folded and put away. It really does become a family affair when everyone is hungry and can smell dinner ready.

More than once our family home evening has begun with a sock fight originated while folding clothes together.

Well-Spent Day

At the end of the day
I look about,
and all the things
I didn't complete
are there for all to see.

While all I did do
goes unnoticed,
even by myself.

The meals consumed,
the clothes in closets,
the listening ear,
the bumps kissed,
the hugs,
the baby smiles on a swing.

At the end of a day
I am tired and discouraged;
The mending still sits,
This room is too cluttered,
The sheets unchanged,
The dust undisturbed.

Dear Lord, please help me remember I am only one person with a
big job. Help me to see what I *did* do as clearly as I now see what I
didn't do so that I may rest through the night in peace after a well-
spent day.

Life Is Much Too Important to Be Taken Seriously

We all know her.

She's actively visible in all six of her church callings. Her cookie jar is always full of fresh, homebaked cookies, and into her kids' lunch boxes she puts sandwiches that look like teddy bears and bunnies.

Her home is "House Beautiful," and in July she begins sewing elaborate Halloween costumes for the family.

She polishes silver and copper and watches the "MacNeil-Lehrer Report" while she irons the sheets.

She organized her city's Fourth of July parade, bakes cinnamon rolls for the Assistance League's welcoming committee, and alphabetizes her spices.

Her six children are all dressed in original, home-sewn designs (spotless, of course), and they all have memorized the thirteen Articles of Faith.

She's Super Mom!

The neighbors will tell you that, the teachers will tell you that, the pediatrician will tell you that, the Relief Society president will tell you that, her children will . . . , her children are not here. They're all at Jimmy's house where Jimmy's mom is sitting on the floor with all the neighborhood kids eating Oreos and playing Bonkers. Life is much too important to be taken seriously.

In our maternal roles we are in a position to give and serve unceasingly. Sometimes we forget that we can't give of ourselves if we are running on empty.

Hiding Out

I'll admit it . . . I've been hiding out.

My going "underground" was triggered by a comment I made on the phone about being so busy that my baby daughter hadn't been bathed by immersion for weeks (or did I say months?).

After I hung up I began to think things over.

Have I been neglecting my family?

A boy with overgrown hair walked into the room, said "Hi, Mom," and headed for the refrigerator.

I knew it must be one of mine (the "Hi, Mom" gave it away), but which one? How long has it been since he had a haircut, and how did he get so tall?

I asked my husband if he felt neglected. He said, "You love your typewriter more than you love me," and broke into pitiful sobs.

As he went out the door, he said, "By the way, my cold is almost gone."

Cold? What cold?

Where's the baby?

I found her in her brother's room sampling Legos.

I found number two son's report card in the back of the camper, two weeks after it had been sent home. I'd never seen it, and it had good grades!

I *have* been neglecting my family. That does it. I may have five church callings to magnify, but I also have five family members that need magnification at a higher power.

I turned on the answering machine. I cancelled my reservations at any meetings that could function without my opinions—virtually all of them.

I taught my three-year-old the names of his eleven cousins (all girls) while we polished the linen-closet doors together.

I held hands and munched popcorn with my husband while we watched his favorite chase scenes.

I watched "The Mummy" with my eight-year-old.

I took a "walk" (twelve miles at four and one-half miles per hour) with my ten-year-old.

I gave my daughter three wonderful splashy baths, for which she indicates appreciation by trying to crawl into the sink every chance she gets.

The answering machine is flashing like Las Vegas, and the mail is threatening to demand it's own room. But I am unaware, wrapped in a protective cocoon of home and hearth. It's been bliss.

I just answered the phone. "Can you please help me out with my Relief Society lesson?"

"Sure!" I surprised her with my enthusiasm. After retreating home for regrouping, I am renewed. My vessel is full and I am ready to give of my surplus.

But I hope and pray that this time I will remember to gauge my giving, and not let my vessel run dry.

How often do we exhaust ourselves with fret, worry, and the anticipation of doom and gloom over something that never materializes?:

On Worrying About the Future

While running errands with Christopher, three, and Kiera, eight months, I stopped in a parking lot to nurse the ever-hungry baby. Christopher peered out of the car's smudged windows and asked questions: "Where are we? What are we doing? Can I go in? I like this store! Can I ride that ride?"

I looked to see what he was talking about.

There it was. A proud black stallion. It's bridle was gold, and from the way it held it's head I could tell it was ready to run.

I took a breath, ready to give my usual answer, "There's no time for that today."

But I stopped myself.

Well, why not? I had a quarter. I could let the little wide-eyed kid tame the black stallion.

We marched solemnly to the impatient stallion. My son mounted with the ease and reverence of an experienced horseman. I got my quarter out.

Our eyes met.

"Wait, Mom! I don't wanna! I'm scared!"

After all I'd had to resolve to get this far, I wasn't about to give up easily.

"You are? Do you want to hold my hand?"

"Yes!"

He held my hand with his right hand and the horn of the saddle with his left. A real cowpoke.

I dropped the quarter in the box. We froze, waiting.

Nothing. *Nothing!*

I pushed the coin return button. Nothing. The proud black stallion had eaten my quarter and would give us nothing in return.

All that fear and anticipation for a horse in suspended anima-
tion.

We walked away. I didn't look back but I noticed my son turn
once. I wondered if he was disappointed or relieved.

Throughout my errands I thought about that horse ride that
never happened and how I sometimes worry about things that never
come to be.

I got a little lesson for my quarter as surely as if it had been
dispensed from the horse's mouth.

I haven't met a parent yet who hasn't learned something from
being a parent. Many parents will agree that they learn plenty from
their children. Sometimes children even have simple but profound
lessons to teach us, if we just pay attention.

I'd Like to Bury My Testimony

I found three-year-old Christopher sitting in bed strumming his
ukelele. He strummed one string and said, "This one's quiet";

strummed the next and said, "This one's sad"; strummed the next string and said, "This one's happy"; then strummed the last one and said, "This one's broken. I need to fix it."

Children, as most of us have discovered, have a refreshing viewpoint, and they express it in quite original ways. Here are more examples from our household:

"Chompstick"—chopstick

"Oceanlotion"—sunscreen

"Flutterby"—butterfly

"Grunchy"—grouchy

"Sour bug"—sow bug

"Wombmates"—twins

Michael was asked where he got his haircut. "The butcher shop," he replied. Later when someone had corrected him, he said, "I meant the barber shop; I always get those mixed up."

When Michael was three and Jason was five, Michael said, "When you cook butter it gets gone." Jason was in school and a man of the world. He confidently and patiently corrected Michael, "No, Michael, not 'gets gone'—it *goes gone.*"

One son requests scrambled eggs, another requests "eggs in the shape they're in."

And most of us have heard children solemnly stand at the pulpit and state, "I'd like to bury my testimony."

But it's that fresh guilelessness that makes them so sensitive to feelings and so observant. So teachable.

My husband was leaving for work, and the whole family was demonstrating exaggerated despair. "Don't go!" we pleaded as we clung to his legs. He left when we were all too weak from laughter to play anymore. As he drove away, our six-year-old son said, "He knows he gets love here."

Then there are the moments like this: Jason was five and we were talking about the still, small voice that tells us right from wrong. I was trying to explain to him how it sounds when he calmly said, "I hear it without my body."

Ah, yes, Jason. How'd you know? But of course you'd know. What else can you teach me?

Autumn . . .

Leaves begin to fall, and mothers begin to reap what they have sown.

Autumn is a period of harvest and maturation. Children reach new heights, physically . . . and otherwise.

Another One Passed Me Up

I'll never forget the time when a friend introduced me to her "little" brother and he towered above her by at least a foot.

Since I had only an older sister and she was a couple of inches taller than I, it hadn't occurred to me that sometimes younger siblings outgrow older ones.

Then it began to happen: my children started outgrowing me! It took me by surprise since my oldest child had stopped growing one inch short of my 5′ 2½″ frame.

The first time I noticed that I was looking *up* into my oldest son's eyes, I just couldn't believe it had happened. I thought he was teasing me *again* by standing on his toes.

My second son was always very small for his age. Somehow it seemed as if it could never happen—he would never outgrow me. But he sure let the whole world know when he did!

And now I find myself looking eye to eye with my youngest daughter. It won't be long . . . Judging by the size of her feet, she will outgrow me by quite a bit.

There's still one son shorter than I, but I know now that the comfort of being able to reach down to rest my hand on his shoulder is short-lived. It is only a matter of time.

Fortunately, I have the one daughter who reached adulthood without growing past me—at least in height. There is a certain sense of security in knowing that she'll always be my little girl.

But probably only in a physical sense. I stand in awe of the stature I see each of my children achieving. Whoever coined the phrase about "giants standing on the shoulders of previous generations" must have experienced the phenomenon of seeing children reach adulthood.

It is good to see my children outgrow me.

For many of us autumn means back-to-school days, but parents never really left.

"The Glory of God Is Intelligence"

"The glory of God is intelligence." As a people we fully embrace the phrase and the philosophy.

But I suspect that when we heard that our earthly existence would be one of learning and testing, we didn't fully comprehend all that it would involve.

Just as a school child looks forward to college without understanding what it will be like, we looked forward to earthly existence with similar idealism.

While a college student groans over the requirement to take chemistry or English literature and then sweats through a challenging final exam, we groan over the noisy debut of a fifth child. We roll our eyes heavenward and mutter, "Give me strength!" But notice how parents who have witnessed the debut of even more children are so much more serene and philosophical. They got their strength with the first half dozen.

As our responsibilities increase, we moan over being called to nurture the nursery, balance the Blazers, or preside over the Primary. "How can I do it?" we implore. "How can I take on more

responsibility?" "Another mouth to feed?" "How can you possibly be out of clean underwear? I did seven loads of laundry yesterday!"

The amazing thing is that each week gets busier than the last, and the challenges get tougher as our earthly education advances.

At marriage we enroll in Intermediate Tolerance.

With the birth of a child we study Patience, and move to Advanced Patience as more babies come.

The novice parents feel there must be a mistake; they aren't ready for the tough lessons required by having a two-year-old. And when the toddler becomes a teenager, they find out what graduate level courses are like.

And they still have to take "Moral Responsibility II," "Family Interaction 200 and 300," "Values 201," and "Advanced Values."

As they progress, there's "A Spiritual Interpretation of Life," "The Ideal Role of a Grandparent," "Joy in Adversity," and an assortment of intensive advanced studies. If the course work doesn't refine us, the homework surely will.

And thus we pass from one learning experience to another, each time growing as we face yet another refiner's fire.

Ask the college graduate if he regrets the all-night study marathons or the physics or philosophy class. Ask if he regrets the years of stretching his mind one more time to fit in Shakespeare and the solar system.

Ask him if he's better for it.

In hindsight we embrace with joy that "the glory of God is intelligence" and that it is not easily acquired.

And now I must let go of the peaceful haven of writing about it, and get back to class. Today I have "Priorities 300" and "Graduate Studies in Patience: A Practicum."

The learning goes on maternally. Mothers never run out of unique learning opportunities. It has been said that some of the best learning comes from the most painful experiences. And what could be more painful than seventh grade, again!

Seventh Grade, Again!

I'm going through seventh grade, again! This is the fourth time. (Actually the fifth, if I'm allowed to count when I did it for myself.) I should know what to expect by now, but it remains a time of great unexpectations.

Whenever any of my friends start to moan and groan about their seventh graders, I nod my head knowingly. "Yes," I tell them, "it is one of the most difficult years. I've always said seventh graders should be put in cold storage for about a year and a half."

This time, however, seventh grade started out so serenely, I had begun to mistrust my memory of the previous encounters. This seventh grader would bounce home each day with glowing reports about the significant happenings of her school day, and I wondered if I was in the right scenario.

She even breezed through the much-dreaded International Report for which our junior high is notorious. (And she chose Russia, to boot.)

The one complaint was that there weren't any Home Economics courses for some unfathomable reason, such as lack of interest. The well-equipped Home Ec room was being used for a study hall.

The teacher who taught Home Ec when my oldest daughter was in seventh grade still teaches at the school, but she is now a science instructor—a sad comment on our society's priorities. What is even more ironic is that my two oldest sons had Home Ec as a required subject during junior high. At least they got the benefit of that preparation for their missions.

We were midway through the school year and I had been lulled into a false sense of security. I was almost sure that I had misjudged seventh graders all these years. Then it happened!

The moods came, the snappy remarks surfaced, talking on the telephone for hours became the norm. *Teenage* a la female had arrived with lavish doses of starving one day to fit into a certain skirt, and going on a cookie-baking binge the next. (And you know that means eating lots of dough!)

She became totally unpredictable. She would swear me to secrecy about something personal and then blab it to everyone at the dinner table herself.

As a sixth grader she wouldn't be caught dead in the junior high clothing department, although size-wise it was the place she needed to shop. She kept telling me that she didn't want to grow up. I tried to talk her into wearing nylons for a special occasion and she wouldn't even consider it.

Now, she won't shop anywhere *but* the teen shop, even when it means paying twice the price for a bathing suit that is exactly the same as one in the girls department.

At first I was a little dismayed by the change, but it didn't take long for me to shift to the familiar early-teen gear.

Seventh grade is such a precarious bridge between childhood and adulthood. Anyone making that uncertain crossing (parent or child) needs good shock absorbers and an extra gear called tolerance. Even though I had been over the road before, I knew I was in for more delightful surprises.

It was comforting to know that this seventh grader was normal after all, even though she still refuses to wear nylons.

Patience. What a paradox. We say in one breath, "Will they ever grow up?" Then we find ourselves observing how much a child has changed, over night. In the next breath we wonder, "*Must* they grow up?"

What would it take for us to be able to fully appreciate the moments we have today?

The Dream

I must have dozed off. I heard a child's voice calling. I reluctantly went to see—what now?

When I opened the door, there was a neat and tidy couch where his crib used to be, a desk where his toy box once stood. And I thought I had heard him calling me.

I went back to my work. I heard an infant's hungry cries. I often think I do. I went to her room. She wasn't there. Where her bassinet once stood, there's a TV and a chair where her pink dresses once hung.

I went to the garage to find evidence that they once existed as chubby infants who needed me. There's the bassinet and the crib, some toys, some tiny shoes. The cast-off shells of the infant.

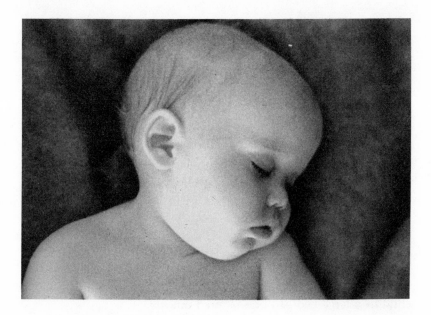

Where are they now? How could they have passed along so quickly, discarding baby things and baby ways? Why was I always in such a hurry to get my important things done? Why was I always in such a hurry for them to grow?

I thought I heard my infant's hungry cries and my son's insistent calling. Then I realized that I *did* hear them, for I had been dreaming in the tired sleep of a mother.

I rushed to them with joy and touched their warm, clinging bodies with gratitude.

I thank thee, dear God, for today.

We don't clearly see our children growing. It's hindsight that provides us with the best view. But all mothers take note of the cast-off shoes and beds.

Sleeping Children

Why is it that a child asleep seems so much bigger than the last time you noticed?

It happens over and over again, with child after child.

One minute the newborn fits the bassinet like a green walnut in its shell—shriveled and undeveloped. In the next moment, the ripened fruit is ready to burst the too-small husk.

It's time to transfer the little "bundle from heaven" to a *huge* crib with the mattress in its highest position. Surely, one thinks, this nightly abode will last a long time, mattress descending to lower positions as necessary.

But months pass, and the growing cherub stops sleeping in that cute scrunched-up baby position. All too soon the crib is inadequate. Toes and locks nearly bump opposite ends as the emerging child stretches out of the cocoon of infancy.

Babyhood recedes and the toddler moves into a *real* bed, complete with top and bottom sheets, blankets, pillow, and a menagerie of stuffed animals. Certainly, this is the end of the mattress march.

However, the false sense of security generated by seeing a small child in a large bed can be shattered quickly.

I went into the room of my youngest offspring one night to cover up the exposed body parts protruding from the disarrayed bedding. The size of the arms, legs, and feet that I saw startled me. I took a closer look. Surely an imposter giant had crept into the bed since I had said good night.

For a moment, I thought the kids might be playing a trick on me by switching beds. I quickly dismissed this idea as the next older child is very territorial and would never condescend to sleep in a bunk bed.

In that darkened room, I had to face a milestone of reality—*I no longer had a small child*. I pondered the miracle of growth that was transforming my children before my unseeing eyes.

"Wasn't it yesterday that they were small . . . ," a familiar tune played in my head as I covered my "baby."

I decided that children asleep look bigger because they are in one place for more than two seconds. Adult eyesight can perceive a child's whole frame more accurately when it isn't a blur of perpetual motion.

But more important, I surmised that sleeping children appear more grown-up because of the peaceful innocence reflected in their faces. Gone are the daytime deceptions and masquerades that tether them in the realm of childhood.

In quiet moments like this, a mother is allowed to glimpse the future stature and noble potential of her sleeping giants.

It has been said that by the time we finally get parenting all figured out, we're out of a job. Even brand-new parents and not-so-new parents have quite different perspectives on the subject. Ah, the pathos of hindsight.

What a Difference a Few Kids Make

I have friends who are first-time parents; their behavior reminds me of myself back then.

I'm not so green now. And not anything at all like a first-time parent, but they don't seem to be aware of our differences.

I know, they're preoccupied.

The green, expectant parent can't wait for the baby to be born. They think it'll be fun to have a baby to make faces at during long sacrament meetings.

The veteran parent can't wait for the chance to sit in silence throughout an entire sacrament meeting talk.

The green parent can't wait till the baby learns to walk and talk.

The veteran parent can.

The green parent rocks the baby, sings a lullabye, and tiptoes around saying "Shhh . . ."

The veteran parent rocks the baby and yells, "What are you guys doing out there?" "Michael, give it back to him!" and "Will someone get the phone?"

The baby of green parents wakes up in a room at the other end of the house, with the door closed, a humidifier humming peacefully, and a recording of the mother's heartbeat constantly playing nearby.

The baby of veteran parents sleeps peacefully on the living room floor in the middle of a birthday party with fourteen four-year-olds breaking balloons.

When the baby of green parents drops a pacifier on the carpet in the Relief Society room, the mother excuses herself to go wash it.

When the baby of veteran parents drops a pacifier in the dog's dish, the mother gives it right back.

The baby of green parents is taken to baby gymnastics, infant learning centers, tot parks, and baby animal petting zoos.

The baby of veteran parents is taken to the third-grade recital, pack meetings, parent-teacher conferences, and temple recommend interviews.

Green parents say, "No-no," "Yuck-yuck," "Tum-tum," and "Binky."

Veteran parents say, "No, you may not play with your brother's chemistry set."

Green parents look at their sleeping baby and say, "Hurry and grow big and strong. Thrive! I have so many plans for you, so much for you to learn."

Veteran parents look at their sleeping baby and say, "How'd you get so big? You're growing too fast. Slow down, little one. I'd like to enjoy your babyhood a little longer. Soon it'll be gone forever and you'll be grown. Let's take it slowly, little one."

There is some loss in watching our children growing up so quickly. But growth can be a matter for rejoicing—it makes the loss of our babies bearable, to watch them change and grow and yet remain beloved individuals.

It's a comfort to know that we can be mothers in the eternities. We will need just about that much time to get it done right.

There are so many books on how to rear children. A mother could spend every waking moment reading them—after she hires someone to rear the children, that is. And she'd still be reading them after her children are bouncing grandchildren on their own knees. But read a few, or even a dozen, if it helps.

Child-Rearing Expertise

I left college armed to the earlobes in child-rearing expertise.

I was calm, confident, capable, and ready.

Then the kids began to check in, and I realized I wasn't ready after all. But by then it was too late.

Nothing in my psychology texts had prepared me for a toddler who would walk up to a menacing motorcycle-gang type and cheerily say, "Hi!" as if it had been Santa Claus with a whole stable full of reindeer bearing gifts.

No professor had warned me about little boys who stick knives into electrical outlets, immersing the house in a sparkling fireworks display.

Nowhere did I study examples of *prenatal* sibling rivalry until I experienced first hand a toddler sitting on what was left of my lap exchanging thumps with his yet-to-be-born brother.

Never did anyone discuss what to do when suddenly your beginning walker has slipped away to begin piano lessons . . . in the middle of your great-aunt's funeral.

Nor would I realize that a child might run down the street before putting on *any* clothes, or return from the beach with a dead squid, or borrow your toothbrush to brush the dog's teeth.

But then none of my studies prepared me for how I'd feel the first time my newborn smiled at me, or everytime I see any of my kids step tentatively onto a stage to sing in a Mother's Day chorus.

How, you might ask, would I rewrite those texts on child rearing, now that I've completed so much "lab" work?

That's simple.

I'd just say, "Love your children. Love them some more. And keep on loving them no matter what."

Now that we won't need to read quite so many books on how to raise our children, let's see what other burdens we may be carrying around needlessly. After all, we have enough of a job to do without making it any more difficult.

The Ten Non-Commandments

I don't know why it took me so long to learn it. Maybe it has something to do with being raised in the Church. All that pioneer heritage, I guess.

Now that there are so many converts in the Church, I am privileged to be exposed to other viewpoints and other life-styles which are equally valid.

As a result I have decided to relieve myself of my burdensome "non-commandments":

1. Bread baking is not a requirement for the celestial kingdom.
2. Children in store-bought clothes will not become juvenile delinquents.
3. Quiltmaking will not make one's calling and election sure.
4. During a temple recommend interview, the bishop does not ask sisters if they have learned to do cross-stitch.
5. Cookies and punch are not mentioned in the Word of Wisdom.
6. The consumption of TVP will not cause a sudden desire to do genealogy.
7. Making elaborate quiet books for my children may not necessarily ensure quiet.
8. Using jam from the corner store will not cause lightning to strike.
9. Putting my three-year-old in a three-piece suit and tie on Sunday will not guarantee that he'll serve a mission.
10. Plastic grapes in the living room do not keep away evil spirits.

There, what a relief. Now I can get on with doing the really important things—followed, of course, by the really enjoyable things. But first I think I'd like my "non-commandments" stitched into a sampler just to remind me.

I'll just have to find someone to cross-stitch it for me.

A mother can list her priorities, and she can eliminate the unessential. But what about her influence?

Positive or negative, ready or not, she teaches and influences. How does she feel about that responsibility?

Mother Education Still Hurts

"There is sunshine in my soul today . . ." The words stuck in my throat as the sisters around me enthusiastically sang the closing song in Relief Society.

It had been another well-prepared, well-presented Mother Education lesson on "A Mother's Influence."

After all these years, I thought, it seems I should be able to sit through these well-meant lessons without guilt setting in. But time hasn't eased my feeling of inadequacy every time I'm reminded of the importance of my influence as a mother.

To top it off, I had been asked to give the closing prayer.

I looked around during the cheery singing, and wondered if any of the other women were struggling with similar feelings. Outwardly, everyone seemed caught up in the spirit of the song.

I know Mother Education lessons aren't meant to be depressing. In fact, I served for two years in the awesome capacity of Mother Ed teacher and thoroughly enjoyed it. Of course, I learned more than the women I taught.

When I had two more children afterwards, I would sometimes refer to them as the ones born A.D. (after direction). Surely the three born B.C. (before coaching) had been short-changed.

But here I was again, feeling flooded with failure as I evaluated my performance against the ideals of the lesson.

Somehow I managed to pray sincerely, asking for our Father's help in implementing the lesson. I don't think anyone noticed the catch in my voice.

Following the prayer, the buzz of voices in the Relief Society room seemed to indicate that "all was well." Maybe I'm on this guilt trip alone, I thought. Maybe I'm the only one who left the breakfast dishes in the sink because I forgot to turn the crammed-full dishwasher on last night.

However, when I think about conversations I've heard in which the "Molly Mormons" and "Patty Perfects" tell it like it is, there is strong evidence that a great disparity exists between the ideal and where most of us are. I decided that most of the women in that room were faking!

So what's the secret of coping with the icepick-in-the-forehead feeling that comes after one of these lessons?

Take two aspirin and lock yourself in your bedroom with a good book and a box of chocolates?

Well, I went home that Sunday, sat down at my word processor, and started a book, while my husband watched the Super Bowl in one room, and the children watched the portable TV in another.

What kind of influence was I having? At least the children were watching "Little House on the Prairie."

Memorizing Moments

Growing each time I turn my head,
Hoping that if I stop and watch
and memorize him
I might have the power to stop time.

Christopher—cherubic, round, soft,
fat, pink cheeks, and soft, silken, buttery tendrils
resting on a soft fat neck.

He'll never again
Be what he is at this moment.
He'll grow into a gangly, freckled boy
with dirt and scrapes and
uncertainties.

They always do.
Nothing I can do will keep a baby there
for long.

Holidays are a time to celebrate family life and to find a balance. The very things we wish to emphasize often become buried under a lot of things that we feel we must do. And the more "must-do's" we have, the less we are able to enjoy our families and the season. Is there a solution that will strike a balance? Well, Margaret had one.

The Dinner

It was Margaret's first Thanksgiving dinner—or at least the first time she had ever had it in her own home. She began to read cookbooks in September.

In October she began to solicit advice.

She asked her mother how to cook the turkey.

"You'll have to get up very early in the morning." Her mother said, "You can use my stuffing recipe; I'll send it to you. It calls for walnuts, you'll have to shell them ahead of time, of course. But don't worry, dear, the important thing is that the family will be all together."

She asked her sister-in-law for a yam recipe.

"Well, I have about four yam recipes," her sister-in-law said. "I'm not sure which one to send you because Bert and Carol don't eat sugar, Grandpa can't have salt, and Mary and Bob are on a low-fat diet. I'll send them all to you. But don't make a big fuss; the meal is not as important as the company. Don't you agree?"

She asked her sister about a salad.

"Whatever you do," her sister said, "don't serve that red gelatin salad Mom always serves. You know how hyper my kids get when they eat that stuff. But do what you want. I'm coming to see my family, and I don't care what we eat."

When she looked at pumpkin pie recipes, her son peered over her shoulder and drooled at the pictures. "Oh boy!" he said. "I love homemade pumpkin pie, and we can roast the seeds too!" She shut the cookbook. Then her son added, "But I learned in Primary that the important thing about Thanksgiving is being grateful for what we have, and being together. Right, Mom?"

Right.

Thanksgiving Day finally arrived, and so did parents, in-laws, aunts, uncles, and assorted cousins.

They were impressed with how cool and collected Margaret seemed for her first Thanksgiving Dinner.

As they sat at the table they looked warily at one another and then at Margaret, who said, "Just peel the foil off your dinner; you'll find a little area for your cranberry sauce in the upper left-hand corner. Your mashed potatoes are on the right, and that larger section has your turkey and peas. If you want more, you can get another dinner from the freezer and microwave it on high for four minutes. The pumpkin pie is thawing out now. And don't forget we came here to be together as a family, and to be grateful for what we have. Right?"

During the harvest years, it often feels good to do a thorough closet cleaning. It's surprising, and sometimes even a little gratifying, to see what emerges from the depths of a son's closet.

It's the Thought

I received a Mother's Day gift from my high school senior around the first of June. Since Mother's Day is the second Sunday in May, one might think he was only a few weeks late—right?

Wrong! He was five years late!

Let me explain. Although we're at a point in our lives where our children are making their own places in the world, we still have a full house. It seems there is always someone in the extended family or "family of the heart" who needs a place to live. Our household seems to be eternally stretchable.

Such was the case one summer when our college son returned from school. His usual room was occupied and he had to share his younger brother's room.

Since we were expecting several sets of company throughout the summer, we were literally bursting at the seams. To alleviate some of the crunch, I ordered a general closet cleaning.

My high school senior was unhappy about my declaration, but I reminded him of certain desired privileges ("You do want to go to the all-night graduation party, don't you?"). Realizing I had that I-really-mean-it tone in my voice, he took a big trash can to his room and went to work.

Because his closet is extra large, it had become a catchall for everyone. It was a veritable treasure trove, and cleaning it turned out to be an adventure for the whole family:

A younger son received a sizable addition to his miniature car collection.

A younger daughter was rewarded with a box of Barbie dolls that had belonged to her older sister. She was very emotional about the fact that the dolls were dressed just as her sister had last played with them before putting them away—*forever.*

We found our older daughter's dried wedding bouquet, now all we need is a place to put it permanently—like at *her* house.

My husband found a set of screwdrivers that had been missing since he built the closet some five years before.

Our oldest son located some of his misplaced mission mementoes. Now he had no excuse not to get them organized into a box labeled "Things to Organize."

Every family member (that wanted any) received a supply of partially used, slightly dog-earred spiral notebooks.

My bonus? Besides some much needed closet space, I discovered it's never too late to receive an almost-finished-seventh-grade-woodshop-project-cutting-board Mother's Day gift. After all, it's the thought that counts.

In the autumn years mothers begin to pay attention to dusty dreams they've been putting aside. Perhaps some will soon be fulfilled, while some will continue to remain in storage until the winter.

Night Time Is the Only Time

Night time is the only time
When it's still and dark
and my mind isn't flitting from
one inconsequential item to the
next, upon demand,
first come, first served.

It's the time for all the poetry
and visions in my head
that have been pushed aside all day
to come out and play.

Like it or not, you know you're in the autumn of maternity when your sons begin to take on more adult-like responsibilities, whether you're ready or not.

Newborn Priesthood

Can it be?
Summer is winding round the last bend. Fall will soon be here. And when fall gets here, so will my eldest son's twelfth birthday! My baby.
The recipient of countless priesthood blessings for tummy upsets, aching gums, skateboarding injuries, and a sprained clavical, as well as receiving a name and a blessing and being baptized, will be eligible for the priesthood himself.
There he will be—scruffed toes, skinned knees, dirt under his nails—and he'll possess the power of the priesthood.

How will I ever concentrate on the sacrament?

I'll be sneaking sidelong glances at him. And I'll be thinking, "Oh, dear, his shirttails are hanging out. I hope he got all the ink off of his hands. I hope he doesn't blow it."

I suppose I'll breathe a sigh of relief when he seats himself after each passing of the sacrament. Perhaps my sigh will grow less audible in time.

I wonder if he'll look different. I wonder how he'll feel.

He already looks different, and I had hardly noticed.

Dear ward members, please be gentle and patient with my brand-new priesthood bearer.

It seems like last week when I walked tentatively into sacrament meeting for the first time with him bundled in my arms. I was nervous about his newborn disturbances—his burps, his wails. Later he crawled up the aisle at the speed of light. You gave me understanding smiles then.

Here we go again.

I present him to you again. This time with his newborn priesthood.

Can it be?

Dear Boys

Around the season that my eldest son was turning twelve, I came across the following excerpt in an old journal:

Sept. 26, 1977

Dear Boys,

In your dark room—Michael, fiddling with your crib toys, and Jason, dreaming dreams of dinosaurs—what would you think if you knew your mother is sitting in the living room half-watching TV, half-folding laundry, and shedding tears because she doesn't want you to grow up and go away. She wants to play "Kitty Cats" and sing "B Is for Bubbles" with you everyday!

All too soon the dinosaur dreaming comes to an end. Little boys turn twelve, then nineteen. It catches mothers by surprise, who will never cease to perceive their sons as little boys with flapping shirttails and ink on their hands.

Missionary Miracles

At age one he was curious about his three-day-old sister napping in the bassinet, so he climbed in and sat on her stomach in order to study her more closely.

At age two he startled his mother, who found him playing on top of the refrigerator.

At age three he set fire to his bedroom.

At age four he decided it was time to go to school so he climbed on the bus. It took most of the day and many parental gray hairs to get him home again.

At age five he decided it was not time to go to school so he threw a tantrum at the bus stop.

At age six he became bored with first grade and visited the third grade just to see what they were doing there.

At age seven he appeared on a children's TV program and told the national audience that his father was "Hop-a-long Cassidy" and that his mother was planning to run away with the circus.

At age eight he had to be baptized three times because he stuck his big toe up out of the water each time.

At age nine he was kept after school for chasing girls.

At age ten he buried his mom's jewelry box in the backyard and charged his friends a dollar each to search for buried treasure.

At age eleven he let his friend's boa constrictor take a nap on his sister's bed.

At age twelve he passed the sacrament in mismatched socks, dangling shirttails, and ink-smeared fingers.

At age thirteen he crashed on his bike while on his paper route and broke his paper-throwing arm.

At age fourteen he stayed after school for chasing girls.

At age fifteen he was taken to the emergency room after being overcome from fumes created by his science project.

At age sixteen he was issued a driver's license.

At age seventeen he fell in love, forever and irrevocably.

At age eighteen he and his BYU roommate became accomplished at creating rockets capable of soaring through the third story windows of John Hall.

At age nineteen he was called to serve a mission, and he accepted and served.

Can there be any doubt that miracles still occur?

Three Hundred Fold

The night we picked up our first returning missionary, I thought I would die from anticipationitis. The fog was rolling in as we drove to the airport, and we worried that the plane might not be able to land.

Sure enough, it happened. We were informed that the plane had arrived and was circling above the airport waiting for a window in the fog. After all the months of separation, it was agonizing to know our son was so close and yet so far.

As we tried to keep family members and friends occupied, my thoughts went back over the months of experiences our missionary had shared in his letters. I could hardly wait to hear the stories firsthand and ask dozens of questions.

He had gone to a poor Central American country and had lived in shacks where the rain beat so hard on the corrugated tin roof that he couldn't sleep at night. Bug-infested outhouses had been the norm. For almost six months he had served in an area in which he slept in a hammock—all the family was anxious for a demonstration of this feat.

One of the delicacies of exquisite cuisine he had encountered included a fish-type chowder called "dulimasi" (which looks like it sounds judging by the picture he showed us).

He also had the opportunity to eat iguana on another occasion. His landlady was very excited to serve it—supposedly a rare delicacy. I was surprised at my heretofore picky eater exulting about eating a lizard! Fortunately, he never had the opportunity to attend a wedding feast, at which a pig's head is the traditional feast.

Then there were the more serious, inspiring stories typical of most missionaries—the golden contact at the last house on the dirt road, the muddy river that cleared up an hour before his first baptism, and baptisms in the surf that turned into free-for-alls because the people were so fun-loving.

My thoughts were brought back to the airport waiting room as an announcement was made that the plane would have to be diverted to another airport. We were told to wait where we were because the passengers would be driven back by bus to go through customs.

After three more hours of waiting, we were told that the passengers were going through customs. Again we waited an eternity, knowing that our missionary was just on the other side of the frosted glass.

At last he came through the doors. It was close to Christmas, and he had a green ribbon and bow draped around himself with a big sign that read "From Santa." It was reassuring to know that his sense of humor was still intact.

Those first few moments of having him home were filled with awe. I wanted to hug him close and stand back and look at him all at the same time. I was sure he had grown two or three inches and his nose seemed longer.

Later when he had finally assured me that he was the same height as when he left, I realized that the illusion was due to a loss of weight. With a feeling of motherly pride, I knew that was something a little home cooking would fix.

Then we got a bonus for our eternity of waiting.

Two Elders who were supposed to fly on to Salt Lake City were stranded because all other flights had been cancelled. They would have to stay overnight. We inherited the strandees.

As we traveled home, tired but happy, it was wonderful to hear the much-anticipated mission experiences firsthand from three young men fresh from the field.

I felt as if we had cast our bread upon the water and it had returned to us three hundred fold.

When our children go on missions, they have new experiences that stretch and strengthen their character.

And when our children marry, we have new experiences that stretch and strengthen our character.

The Right Ingredients

"Good grief!" I kept saying it over and over. I felt a little like a broken Charlie Brown record.

Our daughter had called from college to tell us she was engaged. She had briefly mentioned a blind date in one letter, and that he was a returned missionary in her next letter. Now she was engaged?

"I guess you know what you're doing," I said without meaning it. We hung up with the promise of a Thanksgiving meeting.

We didn't even know what he looked like, but kept reminding ourselves that he must be all right. After all, he was a *returned missionary.* If the ingredients are right, my grandmother used to tell me, the pudding will turn out fine.

Thanksgiving came and went and so did our daughter and her fiancé. He seemed to fit right in and flow with the swift current of our frantic life-style. I kept telling myself the ingredients were right.

The next few months were like a downhill roller-coaster ride. More than once our star-struck couple tried to move up the date. But I exercised my veto power and gave my daughter the same lecture my mother had given me: "Some day it will be your turn to lose a daughter."

The reception was to be at home—a relief since I really didn't want to decorate a cultural hall. Now all I had to do was redecorate the house! It should be easy, I told myself. After all, the ingredients were right.

Christmas shopping that year took a back seat to the wedding preparations. "Here Comes the Bride" was hummed around our house more than "Deck the Halls."

We found the "perfect" wedding dress, the cake and flowers were ordered, and the bridesmaid's dresses were chosen. My youngest daughter was ecstatic about being a flower girl and embarrassed me continually by telling everyone how much her slip had cost!

Even the garden my husband planted was cooperating and the backyard looked lovely. It isn't every wedding that has a vegetable garden backdrop. Again, the ingredients seemed to be right.

The day went smoothly—outside of having the musical number fall through two days before the wedding, having to stay up almost all night to finish last-minute details, and having the groom "missing" at his uncle's house because he was asleep in the wrong bedroom. (It *was* a little disconcerting to have our daughter's almost-in-laws call at 4:30 A.M. to ask if the groom had stayed over at our house, because they couldn't find him!)

Everyone managed to get to the temple on time, however, and the ceremony was beautiful and meaningful. More right ingredients.

The wedding cake must have had the right ingredients, too. I noticed at one point during the reception that there seemed to be plenty, and thought we would have some left over. I hadn't reckoned with the groom's six brothers, who were all in the reception line. Soon after the line disassembled, the cake was gone!

It was several days later when one of my friends who had helped serve punch shared the fiasco that had transpired in the kitchen. The punch bowl was almost empty and she went to the freezer to get a carton of the frozen fruit puree punch base. She took out a plastic container that looked as if it was the right stuff. As she mixed it with the soda, she thought it looked a little strange, but began to serve it anyway.

She had served quite a few guests before someone discreetly suggested she taste the punch. She nearly gagged. The rest of that batch was quickly dispatched down the drain. No one could explain the foul taste.

I realized immediately what had happened. The plastic container didn't hold pureed fruit, it was full of chicken broth left over from stewing chickens. That batch of punch definitely did not have the right ingredients—*fowl* was a good description.

No one else ever mentioned the strange punch we served. (And no one asked for the recipe, either!) I suspect everyone was too polite to say anything, but I'll bet some of our garden got watered with

chicken broth punch that day. Maybe that's the explanation for our unusually good crop of string beans that year?

The garden and the marriage both flourished—a sure sign of the right ingredients.

Where would mothers of sons be without miraculous intervention? Perhaps every son comes equipped with a guardian angel at birth and then is assigned another as he leaves the nest.

Out of the Nest and Onto the Freeway

As a young mother I looked forward to the day when my children could drive themselves where they needed to go.

I even made it through my first two drivers without serious consequences. (My hair had already started turning gray long before!)

We did lose a cat under the wheels of the car my oldest daughter was driving, but we rationalized that she did the old guy a favor since he was literally on his last legs.

And she only had one fender bender, which scared the wits out of her—and us.

Our oldest son, cautious and conservative, was a "Granny" behind the wheel. I had a hard time being patient when he was learning to drive, because he went so slow. (Little did I realize what a blessing that was.)

Last year marked the beginning of our third child's career on motorized wheels. This was an entirely new story.

Agile, coordinated, a total athlete—that's our number three. But three wasn't a lucky number! By the age of three he had already been to the emergency room three times.

He has had more broken bones than everyone else in the family put together. We had more calls from distraught neighbors than any other parent in the neighborhood to come pick up the pieces because he had fallen off his bike in front of their houses. The school nurse knew our phone number by heart.

As the time approached for him to take driver training, I really got nervous. He was still running into street signs and parked cars on his bike. How could we trust him behind the wheel of a car?

Sensing that he wasn't quite ready to graduate to the "big time," he contented himself with a learner's permit for more than a year. He also signed up for two sessions of driver training.

However, at age sixteen and a half, he began to rattle the car keys a little louder. He already had earned his Eagle Scout rank, so we couldn't use that "carrot" to keep him from behind the wheel as some of our friends were doing with their teenage sons.

He even surprised us by getting a B average that semester. Stripped of all excuses, we had to break down and take him for his driver's test.

He was used to driving our big, old, automatic-transmission station wagon. The left side of it was bashed in and the door on the driver's side wouldn't open. This was an embarrassment to him— especially since he hadn't done it. We rationalized about not fixing it since he was driving the car.

He couldn't use this station wagon for the test. Our other car was a stick shift, and he hadn't mastered it sufficiently to use it. Consequently, we borrowed Grandma's vintage Dodge. On the way to the Department of Motor Vehicles I kept reminding him that if he would drive it like the little old lady it was used to, he would probably do fine. He passed the test with flying colors.

Since he hadn't had a lot of experience behind the wheel and especially not alone, we figured he would be content to drive us back and forth to church on Sunday for a while longer and continue using his bike for the rest of his comings and goings. After all, biking fit into his athletic training.

We were in for a rude awakening.

Feeling complacent that everything was under control, I left for Utah with the two younger children to help our oldest daughter move. It just happened that my husband was involved in a project that required his working late at night both days of the weekend.

Before leaving, I had arranged a ride for our athlete to a Saturday swim meet because it was quite a distance away. He didn't feel ready to tackle the freeway system alone, especially with the stick shift.

We had determined that he could drive himself to church on Sunday and figured that it would be a good opportunity for his first "solo."

Fate stepped in. Friday evening he received a phone call telling him of a job opportunity at Disneyland. He would need to attend a four-hour audition early the next morning.

Unable to reach his dad, he called me in Utah. He wanted to know how to get to Disneyland! We had been there dozens of times, but he didn't know how to "drive" there!

Trying to sound calm, I described the route from long distance, including the on and off ramps of the freeway. After the audition he would have to drive on to the swim meet some distance further. It would involve more freeway driving plus an interchange.

I felt like a mother bird pushing her chick out of the nest before its wings were fully feathered.

As I helped my daughter and son-in-law move the next day, my thoughts were far away, wondering how my "accident-about-to-happen" son was navigating the Southern California freeways by himself in the stick-shift car.

At the end of the day when the anxiously anticipated call came, he had a happy report. He had gotten the job, had bettered his times at the swim meet, and had only stalled the car twice. His voice was exuberant with success as he told me he had driven a total of sixty miles.

I knew this was one chick who would never again be content with a bike after learning to fly.

In the autumn season time moves more swiftly. And it takes on an added dimension as we become more aware of our connections to other generations.

Time

"I thought this one might interest you," my mom said, as she handed me an old camera.

Without intention I've accumulated several antique cameras, most found in family garages. Since I'm a shutter bug, they've been passed on to me.

The camera she handed me was not quite as old or as worn as the ones that peer out from shelves in my office. This one had belonged to my grandmother. As I examined its twin lenses I discovered it contained a half-exposed roll of film.

It intrigued me in a restless sort of way. What had my grandmother photographed last, before she carefully put it away in it's leather case?

I finished the roll with photos of my little ones. Children whom she had not had the opportunity to photograph were now reflected onto the emulsion next to whatever or whomever she had chosen to preserve.

While the film was at the lab, I got a phone call from a familiar sounding voice from my past, "Guess who this is?" It was Kris, my first college roommate nearly two decades ago. We arranged to get together soon. The day came. As we visited, we found we were still bound by common concerns. We watched our children play. Our youngest, beginning walkers, were knocking each other down in their attempts to hug each other.

"Wouldn't it be something," Kris said, "if they end up being college roommates like we were?"

It would be something. And when I thought of the film at the lab with its generation-apart exposures, I realized it would not be at all impossible.

When the film came back I found black-and-white prints of myself as a child on vacation with my brothers and sister, doing the kinds of things on the edges of river banks and bridge railings that made my grandmother nervous.

And there was my mother, at just about the same age I am now.

Once again I was impressed, amazed, and baffled by time. It moves on silently, swiftly, forever. But as it moves straight ahead, it leaves an intricate connecting pattern like a carefully worked tapestry.

And sometimes, just for an instant, I get an eternal perspective of time.

We want our children to grow into strong individuals. No mother, given the choice, would actually choose to thwart the progress. Nevertheless, we lament the swiftness of the growing season. It's only natural to want to preserve those fleeting moments. We attempt preservation by memorizing, photographing, cherish-

ing, and recording all that we can. If we could, we'd preserve our
harvest of moments in bottles that we could store in neat rows on a
shelf.

Bottled Moments

"How time flies!" "Why it was only yesterday . . ."
I used to hate to hear *old folks* talk that way.
Even though I was small for my age, people would always
admonish my parents, "Better put a brick on her head; she'll be
grown up before you know it."
Now I find myself almost panicky as I realize how quickly time
has flown, and how close to grown-up my own children are.
In an attempt to hold back The Clock, I wrote "Bottled Moments" some years ago to help me remember my five children as
they were at one moment in time.
How grateful I am to have preserved them during the fullness of
my summer season. This is one "bottled" harvest that will remain
on my memory shelf as my summers fade into autumn.

Summer 1976

One day I observed my thirteen-year-old son, Scott, as he carefully and intently scrutinized a ladybug feeding on aphids on the
yellow rose bush outside our kitchen window.
Fully absorbed in the insect's activity, he was unaware of me or
anything else around him. I studied his clear gray eyes, round
freckled cheeks, "Popcycle" T-shirt, patched and grass-stained jeans,
and falling-apart tennis shoes.
What a story it all told! I wished that I could preserve him in that
moment forever. "How typical he is of boys his age," I thought. "So
intense and complex, so lovable, yet so resistant to Mother's hugs."
On the floor at my feet was eight-month-old Wayne, rolling
around in that not-quite-ready-to-walk mode, completely involved
in his own movement. The sounds of the bells he was playing with
combined with his squeals of delight to fill the room with music.
"So simple, so lovable, and still responsive to Mother's hugs," I
thought. I wished I could hold him in that moment forever. Only
yesterday Scott had been my roly-poly, curly-headed baby boy.

One Sunday in sacrament meeting I was fast losing patience with not-quite-three-year-old Jennifer Joy as she squirmed on my lap. I found myself wondering why I had given her such an inappropriate middle name!

I glanced down the bench at fifteen-year-old Michelle, thinking maybe she would like to trade Wayne for Jennifer for a few minutes. (Dad was in the bishopric during this season of my life.)

My heart skipped a beat as I beheld my eldest in that moment of revelation. I saw a beautiful, well-groomed young woman, wearing a lovely dress she had sewn for herself, ably handling her baby brother. With a tear in my eye I realized that I could no longer hold her on my lap, and I felt a surge of gratefulness for squirmy, loving Jennifer Joy. I hugged her close—hoping to savor that moment just a little longer.

Caught in between the world of babies and teenagers is our toothless wonder, almost-eight-year-old Paul. How priceless are the photos that capture him singing "All I Want for Christmas Is My Two Front Teeth."

Full of pranks and "jack-o-lantern" grins, he is in a state of perpetual motion—on land or in water.

So fun, so lovable, I thought, *but far too slippery for Mother's hugs.* It would be impossible to bottle him in a particular moment, because he just isn't there long enough.

As I finished writing this bottled delight, I realized that there was no way I could stop the ticking. But at least for these few recorded moments, the fruits of my labor are preserved at the peak of my summer season—forever.

Winter . . .

A time to draw the family close for warmth; a time of endings, with the promise of renewal.

Winter brings perhaps the most radical changes, at least in most parts of the United States.

The winter maternal season also brings with it something as fresh and awesome as new fallen snow—grandmotherhood.

Inevitable Evolution

Grandmothers get younger every year! This observation seemed particularly apparent on the eve of my own grandmotherhood!

We had thought of telling our friends that our twenty-two-year-old daughter was adopted at the age of ten and wasn't really our natural child, but she looks so much like her dad that no one would believe us.

I suppose I could tell people that she is "his" daughter by a former marriage, but that doesn't seem fair. Besides, it doesn't give me a chance to take any credit for the beautiful young woman she has become.

Once she was married, which was an adjustment in itself, we began preparing ourselves for the next inevitable step in life's progression—becoming grandparents.

With children who are trying to be obedient to the tenets of the gospel, it usually doesn't take long. We weren't too surprised when the announcement came wrapped as a Christmas gift. What did cause me to choke a little was receiving a customized "grandmother-to-be" Mother's Day card in May from my husband. Of course I retaliated on Father's Day.

And then there was the shock of seeing "our little girl" pregnant! Because we live some distance away, we hadn't been able to grow into the idea. At the time of the initial announcement, she was still skinny. We didn't see her again until she was seven months along.

I thought she looked *huge* for seven months, but I couldn't tell her that. Besides, she made me promise to tell all the folks back home that she wasn't really big at all.

Somehow we made the drastic mistake of predicting that the baby would be born either right on time or even a little early. "Someone" had read "somewhere" that short women have their babies early. Since our daughter is 5' 1", we felt reasonably sure that she would qualify.

At four days overdue, she felt betrayed and another "old wives' tale" bit the dust!

Finally the call came, appropriately on Labor Day, and only ten days late. Another generation had begun.

Once we knew mother and son were fine, I was on the phone making a plane reservation.

Boarding the plane, I was suddenly aware of all the *real* grand-motherly and grandfatherly people around me. Sweet-faced, white-haired, bespectacled men and women seemed to be everywhere. I glanced in a mirror to see if, suddenly, I had been transformed to fit the image of my new status.

I wished I had been wearing a button declaring, "I'm a Grand-mother!" That surely would have surprised them all—maybe.

After all, I still had young children at home. I monitored my diet—and hair color. I exercise every day—if allowed to count running up and down the stairs a dozen times in the course of a normal day's activities.

As the engines of the plane revved, my heart and thoughts followed suit. I eagerly anticipated what it would be like to hold that first grandchild—an extension of myself one generation forward.

I wrote in my journal while waiting for take-off: "From where I'm seated, I cannot see out of the plane. It gives me the feeling of flying into the unknown—and that's just how I feel about grandmother-hood. I'm taking off into a big unknown.

"What I *can* see is that this inevitable evolution is another precious link in the chain of eternity."

Grandmotherhood may indeed be an inevitable evolutionary journey into the unknown. But by the time we reach that season, we are blessedly equipped to sense what matters . . . and what doesn't.

Barefoot Bliss

I was looking for my shoes—again. "What is the matter with me," I thought. "I never used to misplace my shoes; I hardly ever take them off except to go to bed."

I decided my barefoot personality was emerging. (Or is it bare-foot mentality?)

Like most kids, I loved to go barefoot as a child. In the summer, the warm dirt on our farm-like homestead felt smooth and silky sifting through my toes as I watered our various crops.

Sometimes going barefoot meant dashing across stretches of scorching hot pavement to reach the welcome coolness of grassy parks. It meant summer—lie back, read a book, watch the clouds.

Then practicality set in. High school, work, college, more work, and then marriage and children all changed my life-style. About the only time I went barefoot was in the shower or swimming pool.

Our neighborhood is quite urban and not as conducive to going without shoes as were my childhood days. It seems as if I have spent my child-full years reminding my children to put their shoes on. "You might step on something" and "It's too cold to go barefoot" were grooved into my automatic response tape.

Lately I've noticed a change. I find myself kicking off my shoes and leaving them wherever I happen to be.

I've rediscovered the freedom of walking barefoot, not neces-sarily out in the dirt or grass, but even on our carpet with its five-dollars-a-yard plush pad we "had to have" it is an exhilarating experience. It induces a relaxation that just isn't there when feet are confined in shoes.

Whether it's my barefoot personality or mentality coming out, I do know that I've finally reached a point in my life where I can say "I don't care" to the things that really don't matter.

Ah! The bliss of being barefoot again.

Often enough it takes generous seasoning all the way through the winter season of mothering to be certain of the simple things that matter most.

Eternity

I don't want picture-perfect doll children
in sailor blue and organdy.

I don't want a swimming pool and
upstairs and downstairs too.

And two TVs (or more) and
no-wax floors and new decor.

I don't need Volvos and silver
and designer stuff.

I don't care about lights and nights
and party talk.

All I want is you and me
and a flower or two,
a walk on sea-sprayed sand,
tickled toes,
a lick of ice cream,
your crinkled nose.

You and me:
friends, lovers,
perfecting teamwork
and an eternity to do it in.

The view from a mother's winter season is very different indeed. It's been a long climb to get to where she is, but the view makes the climb worthwhile.

And older, wiser eyes are more appreciative of the view.

My Neighbor's Child

A splotch of bright red movement caught my eye through the blinds. I looked out of the window next to my desk and watched my neighbor's little girl running along the street in the late afternoon breeze, the kind of half run, half skip that is characteristic of four-year-olds.

She was alone and thoroughly caught up in her own movements. She would turn her head from side to side and the gusts of light breeze would toss her fine straight hair first to one side of her face and then to the other.

I looked down on her as she raised her face into the breeze. I could see an expression of rapture on her round, still babyish face as she played tag with the wind. The low-lying sun backlit her golden-brown hair, and she looked like an ad for tissue softness.

She was wearing a red dress and on her feet were white socks with ruffled cuffs, no shoes. The socks were still quite white, so I could tell the shoes had been cast off only a short time before.

The innocence and bliss of the scene took my busy mind away from the work I had been doing, and I took a moment's reverie.

It had been many years since my own little girls ran and played in such a carefree way. I wondered if my neighbor appreciated the beauty of the moment.

Thinking back a few years, I remembered that the first thing I would have seen through my young mother's eyes would have been my child's socks, bound to be ruined through carelessness.

"Where are your shoes?" The mother's anxious voice coming from the house verified my theory.

How sad that often only older eyes can appreciate the difference between careless and carefree.

Across Generations

Two sets of eyes
gazing at one another,
Across generations.

Grandmother, here is
your progeny—
A tiny bud, not yet blossomed.
You are teaching, guiding
Across generations.

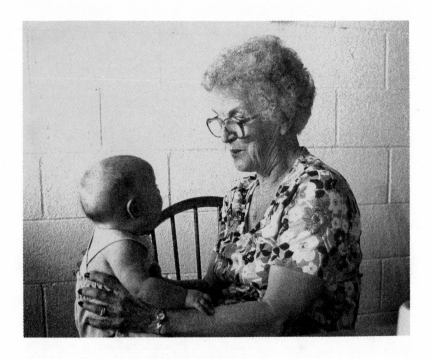

Very little girl, here are
your roots—
Look into her eyes that see
Across generations.

Always

"Once a mother, always a mother."

As my children have matured, I've gained new insight into the meaning of this phrase. Mothering spans the generations. I'm wondering just how far into the eternities a mother's influence will continue.

You know mothering goes on forever when:

—Your grandmother still tells your mother how to cook the macaroni.

—Your mother complains that *your* hair is getting too gray.

—Your married daughter calls long distance to tell you that her kitty has run away.

—You still wait up for a twenty-three-year-old returned missionary.

—You find another mother on the fourth grade field trip who has more grandchildren than you.

—The conversation with a group of friends centers on concern for not-yet-married sons.

—You find yourself fascinated, once more, with "Sesame Street" as you watch it with a grandchild.

—You keep asking your working married daughter when her husband is going to get a job.

—You keep asking your home-for-the-summer son when he's going to get a job.

—You attend Girls Camp with your youngest daughter and find that some of her contemporaries are grandchildren of some of your contemporaries.

—Your children, too old for allowances, still need occasional financial backing.

—You worry about your adult children not taking life seriously enough.

—You worry about your married children taking life too seriously.

The seasonal winter brings with it a time of holidays and special family warmth. Maternal winter offers time for remembering those times of celebration, joy, and unexpected lessons.

Confection Perfectionist

I must have been daydreaming. I saw myself in a gingham apron surrounded by worshipful, apple-cheeked children and the aroma of bread and cinnamon.

It's those women's magazines. The Christmas issues get to me every time! All those lavish gingerbread houses, and the Christmas decorations painstakingly fashioned from discarded milk jugs and juice cans that had been saved, supposedly, all year long just for Christmas.

I succumb to their lure only once a year when Christmas baking, decorations, parties, and even clever gift wrapping become equated with love (in my mind or the magazine's, I'm not sure which, but I have my suspicions).

So I pore over those Christmas issues like a college freshman opening brand-new geology and sociology text books, with a mixture of dread and excitement.

Oh, no. They won't get me to stay up till midnight finishing a Victorian gingerbread house just because I love my kids. One of them would probably sit on it anyway.

And I am certainly not interested in putting together that wreath with 28,300 gum wrappers folded into intricate patterns and spray-painted gold, even though I could surely come up with the correct amount of gum wrappers by cleaning the boys' room. That's not love, that's obsession.

But the daydream persists. It is, after all, Christmas; and these are, after all, little children. I am responsible for their memories! Do I want them to tell my grandchildren about how I stopped off at the bakery on Christmas Eve? Are you kidding? I want them to wax poetic as they reminisce about the smells of evergreen and cloves and the taste of homemade goodies. These are warm manifestations of their mother's love, right?

The daydream returns. I see a patient, sweet mother in the kitchen with her children. They are making Christmas cookies together. One apple-cheeked boy has a smudge of flour on his button nose. Dad comes home and the scene before him fills his heart with joy. Now isn't that what Christmas is all about?

In an attempt to play the daydream out in real life I announce, "We're going to make Christmas cookies!"

My number one son says, "Aw, Mom, I want to go to Roger's; he's got video games."

The rest of the children shout "Goodie!" with so much glee that I wonder if they shouldn't be locked out of the kitchen.

I get out the flour. I get Christopher out of the flour. I get the flour out of Christopher's hands. I ask Michael to get the flour off the floor.

I get out the cookie cutters. I wash the playdough off the cookie cutters. Jason gets the rolling pin from the sandbox.

Finally we have the dough mixed. Half of it, however, has "mysteriously" disappeared.

Christopher holds up a gob of dough. "Can I eat this?"

I sigh, "You may as well."

He says, "Why?"

Jason rolls the dough. I answer the phone.

Christopher asks, "Why do I have to eat this?"

Michael says, "Mom, he's not letting me have a turn!"

The baby cries. I go to change her.

In the kitchen I hear the kind of commotion that makes mothers want to slip out of the back door.

I take a deep breath and go back.

I see raw cookies everywhere. Some are even on the cookie sheet, a few even cut with cookie cutters. Apparently that wasn't creative enough—the remainder have been formed by hand into oddly shaped monstrosities.

"This is a snake!"

"This is a monster!"

"This is Jabba the Hut!"

And I was going to wrap these gifts from our kitchen in gold foil and merrily deliver them to the neighbors.

I abandon all plans except for making it through the evening.

Frosting time has arrived and I'm gone again, putting the baby to bed. My three-year-old is following me around with that original piece of dough, "Is it good for me if I eat this?"

I decide that if I take out my contact lenses it will soften the shock of what I'll see when I return to the kitchen. I take another deep breath and plunge back in. When I left we had mixed several colors of frosting. Now all the cookies are being frosted with one color—a grayish green—which is, I am informed, "what you get when they're all mixed together."

I am weary of well doing. I rush the kids off to their beds and clean up.

Oh well, I can always stay up until midnight making banana bread for the neighbors.

Finally it's quiet. I look at those magazines again. Obviously their test kitchens don't include children. That would be a *real* test kitchen.

Three-year-old Christopher calls from the darkness. He wants a drink. I bring him into the kitchen. He puts his arms around my neck and asks, "Did you see my cookies?"

I tiredly nod, "Yes."

He says, "My Mary?"

"Your what?"

I look at the grayish blobs where he points.

"I made Mary and Joseph and the baby Jesus."

I look again and begin to see the forms shaped by his pudgy hands.

"Yes, I see, Christopher . . . they're wonderful."

We give each other a goodnight hug.

I put him to bed and come back out and throw out those magazines.

Christmas Story

I wanted the shopping trip to be perfect. That's why I planned it two weeks in advance. No more last-minute, slip-shod gift giving by any of my kids . . . no way.

I sat them down and had them make lists. Oh, sure, they groaned about it. But if they didn't make lists, it would be just like all the other Christmases.

One would go off to a shopping center with six dollars and spend a dollar twenty-five on gifts for two parents, three siblings, four grandparents, and one dog, and spend the remaining four seventy-five on gum and darts for himself.

The other would be conned out of most of his allowance by his brother. And another would lose his money down the heater vents.

I took their allowance—carefully sorted into labeled envelopes—their lists, and them, to the mall.

"Maul" would be a better name for it.

Christmas is for families but Christmas shopping is better accomplished by individuals—unless you're willing to invest in some mountain-climbing equipment and leash the family all together. Even my daughter in a large stroller got separated from me when I removed my hand to look at the list.

My four-year-old got stuck at the top of an escalator after a sudden attack of escalator-phobia. My one-year-old nearly got us

arrested when she "shoplifted" a bottle of nail polish—it was an awful shade too. My eight-year-old kept twenty people waiting while the clerk counted out his seven dollars and twenty-nine cents in change, mostly pennies.

Shopping en masse was not working. Instead, I'd wait outside each store with my sticky-fingered daughter while two boys at a time would enter to shop. They'd come out and I'd inspect.

"What's this comic book for?"

"That's for Daddy."

"I thought you were getting him that pen that writes in three colors."

"I couldn't find one."

"What are these baby booties for? They're too small for Kiera."

"Christopher bought those."

"Michael! You shouldn't've let him."

"Mom! He started to cry in the middle of the store. He says they're for the baby Jesus."

"Okay," I sighed.

No, I decide. It's better than okay. Christopher's got a lesson to teach us. As I wait for Jason to come out I begin to imagine the possibilities of Christopher's lesson. We'll keep the booties for every Christmas; we'll put them under the tree or maybe by the Nativity scene. It will be an important family tradition. What a great idea!

Feeling full of fresh Christmas cheer, I let the kids take a cheese and cracker break. As we munched, a very-large-with-child young woman sank wearily onto a nearby bench.

Michael whispered loudly. "Mom? Is that lady going to have a baby?"

She heard, "Yes . . . pretty soon."

"A Christmas baby? Like baby Jesus?" Christopher asked. The woman smiled.

Christopher studied her for a long time.

Finally she got up to finish her shopping and Christopher ran after her with his baby booties.

"Here," he panted, "for the baby."

I wanted the shopping trip to be perfect. But I really didn't know what a perfect shopping trip it would be . . . until that moment.

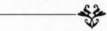

The following story is fictional. I wrote it because the great-grandmother is how I'd like to be when I am coming to the end of the winter season of my mortality; calmly facing an unfamiliar renewal with faith; at peace; savoring the moments with a loving heart; looking closely at my life and realizing, with gratitude, that I have everything and more; and giving what I've kept, treasured and fashioned from my own talents, to those I love.

Christmas Presence

I hadn't seen my grandmother in five years; she simply lives too far to visit often. It was her ninety-fourth Christmas and my mom wanted everyone to be together.

My grandmother had never seen our new baby daughter. She was great-grandmother to eleven little boys, so this baby was special just by being a girl.

When we arrived, there was much commotion inside and outside. My mom hurried about in the kitchen. I looked for my grandmother, anxious to introduce my sweet daughter to her and to ask my grandmother what she'd like for a Christmas gift.

I found her in the living room. She sat gazing at the brilliant Christmas tree, humming along to the carols playing on the stereo.

I started to approach her, but something stopped me. There was a tear glistening on her smiling face. I backed up silently. I dared not intrude with my conversation. My daughter was quietly entranced with the tree. The three of us seemed connected by the quiet. I decided to ask her later.

At dinnertime my grandmother appeared. She walked straight to my daughter, her face beaming with joy. Gently she lifted her in her arms and slipped into a corner chair to murmur her loving grandmother language. My daughter cooed and smiled in reply. I decided to ask her after dinner.

Several days passed and I still didn't know what I'd give my grandmother. I wanted it to be something very special. Something she would truly cherish. Every time I meant to ask her, she seemed busy or preoccupied.

She was listening to little boys' absurd stories, laughing at their silly behavior, telling them stories, or singing carols.

She rocked my baby to sleep every chance she got. She braided my sister's hair, lovingly and slowly, watching it catch the light.

Every time she approached me, she put her arms around me and leaned against me. I'd ask her then, "What can I give you for Christmas, Grandma—something special?"

She'd just change the subject or find someone who needed her right away. One time she looked me in the eyes with a serious, pleading look that gave me a chill, and said, "No, no, child. I *have* everything . . . and more."

Christmas Eve came and there sat my grandmother, reading a story to many grandchildren. She read slowly, savoring the words and the children's reactions.

There I sat, wondering. Maybe a good book, she loves to read. I felt uncomfortable as if pondering an unsolved puzzle.

Christmas morning came. The first thing I saw was a gift-wrapped wad next to my pillow. I opened it and found my grandmother's brooch. I looked at my sleeping daughter. At the foot of her crib lay a box wrapped in a hand-knitted baby blanket. Inside

the box, wrapped in tissue, I found the hand-embroidered baby dress my grandmother had made for me at my birth.

I slipped out of the door and found similar packages carefully placed next to sleeping heads and feet all over the house.

I went to my grandmother's room and found her door slightly opened. I peeked inside and saw her sitting in bed. On her lap was her Bible, stuffed full of children's notes and dandelions. Her head rested on her pillow. Her eyes were closed and she smiled. She was very still.

My father turned on some Christmas music and then came to stand in the doorway behind me. And I heard myself say, "She's gone now, but it's all right. She has everything . . . and more."

Winter is a time for gratitude. And a lot of gratitude is expressed for a second chance. Just look at the popularity of making New Year's resolutions.

Resolution-ing—But Can I Make It Through January 1st?

Finally! The kids are ready for bed. I thought I'd never get the baby to sleep. At last I can jot down my New Year's resolutions. Let's see . . .

1. I must learn to be more patient. A.S.A.P.

2. I resolve to speak in pleasant tones. *"You guys quiet down in there! Do you hear me?"*

3. I resolve to pay more attention to my husband. *(Ring)* "Hello? Hi, honey. Uh-huh. I'm right in the middle of something, can I call you back? Okay. Bye."

4. I resolve to make my family a higher priority. *"Christopher! I'll be there in a minute!"*

5. I resolve to have more empathy for others. *"Not again! I'm coming!" I can't believe he interrupted me for that! He calls me all the way back in there because his toe was uncovered and he couldn't find his teddy bear!*

6. I resolve to be a better time manager. *(Ring)* "Hello? Hi . . . fine, and you? Next Thursday? Hold on, let me look. All I have on Thursday is between one and two p.m., will that be okay? It will? Alright, I'll see you then." I resolve to be a better time manager by getting a smaller appointment book!

7. I resolve to be better organized. *"I thought you were in bed! If you can't find a matching pair of socks, look in the unmatched socks box!"*

8. I resolve to be kind and friendly to others. *"Why aren't you in bed yet? If you can't find any socks I guess you'll just have to get up early in the morning and do a load of laundry. Now get in bed and stay there!"*

Now where was I? All those interruptions! What do I have on my list so far?

I'll have to admit that what I have so far are eight broken resolutions and the ink hasn't even dried yet.

Well, it's New Year's Eve, after all, a good time for fresh starts.

1. I resolve to try to be a better person by paying attention to and taking advantage of all the lessons that present themselves to me hourly and daily within my own walls.

2. Enjoy.

I think it's going to be a good year after all.

Our eternity is made up of good and bad days, and of good and bad years. Minutes, days, years, and decades become shiny pearls and rustic seeds strung along an individual chain of our own design. A chain that is never ending.

The Bridge Through the Mist

Here we stand on the edge
of the bridge.

We nod to acquaintances
and clutch our little ones.

And see the bobbing heads of humanity
stretching all the way to the mist.

We cannot see beyond the mist,
and are tearful when
a loved one disappears from our sight
and fearful as we near it.

What will become of us?
Does the bridge end?
Do we drop off the edge
into icy rapids
never to be seen again?

Do we dissolve into mist?
What becomes of us, all of us,
as we walk along?

"It goes on!" someone whispers.
"I know because I saw
beyond the mist.

I saw my grandmother
and her grandmother too.

They were walking together.
The destination lies beyond the mist."

"Can it be true?" whispers a hopeful voice.

"Let's join hands," whispers another.

Sister to sister, brother to brother,
father to son, mother to daughter,
husband to wife—

We join hands that cross the bridge through the mist,
Into eternity.

Into eternity we march. And all along the way we are fulfilling our obligations. We are busy with well-doing and serving. Perhaps too busy.

To truly esteem others we must take time to develop esteem and acceptance for ourselves.

To serve as mothers, the most demanding service of all, we must nurture ourselves. One way that we can do that is to be true to ourselves, true to the kind of mother that we are. And open to the on-the-job lessons available to us.

Motherhood is the richest role with the widest spectrum of experience. Mothers have much opportunity to enrich and to be enriched. And just when we think we've run out of resources, enrichment comes from an unexpected source—a bubbly smile from a newborn, a toddler singing hymns in the next room, or a sticky hug around the knees. Sometimes it is our children who elevate our motherhood to a lofty place.

But it can also be the pits.

If all women go about with a "I-can-do-it-I-can-do-it-all-hurry-along-now" facade, it builds walls between us.

We need to individualize our roles. There is no perfect mother. There are no perfect children. Just different, dedicated mothers. And terrific . . . terrible children (alternating hourly).

What kind of mother are you?

Do you listen to music and hum while you dust?

Do you dust?

Do you get on the floor and wrestle with your kids?

Are you a sweet and dignified mother?

Are you one kind of mother at church on Sunday and another kind at home on Monday?

If we try to be baking-sewing mothers when we are really tree-fort-building mothers, we deny ourselves joy and we are not able to fully serve our families with joy. And if we are too busy attempting to be the model mom, we won't have time to pause and learn from the resources that surround us, especially our children.

I recently came across the following excerpt in an old journal of mine:

"I am trying to keep up with the dailiness where I am expected to have myself and my family ready for each hour's appropriate obligations, . . . keeping my creative drives and curiosities in pouches I carry, . . . like a child trying to hide a frog in his pocket. Every so often there's some croaking or some escaping and that's fun, but it's back in the pocket again . . . shh . . .

"Sometimes dailiness makes me deeply unhappy. Same old stuff . . . now smile, pretend it's interesting.

"Sometimes dailiness is more wonderful than anything—burying my nose in a baby's neck to enjoy 'baby musk'; touching the skinny bones of my children; the satisfaction of clean, folded clothes; a clean kitchen again; giggles; morning crispness."

Does that sound like anyone you know?

Sometimes it seems as if children, hiding frogs in their pockets, are here to remind us to be true to our "creative drives and curiosities." They remind us to play and to sing. And when we do some playing we are better at the working.

Children also remind us to cry when we are sad and to laugh out loud with joy.

In order to enjoy the wonderfulness, we need to be able to accept the awfulness. If we deny the existence of problems or not-so-cheery feelings, we will lose our ability to feel the joys as joyously as we can.

We need each other—sisters, husbands, sons, and daughters. We need parents, brothers, and grandparents. We are woven together in a tapestry of love, tears, laughter, frustration, and joy. Every one of us has lessons to learn from those ahead of us and those we lead as we travel through our maternal seasons.

We're in this together as we join hands and cross that bridge into eternity.